T0294092

Also available at all good book stores

9781801500630

9781801500067

9781785316470

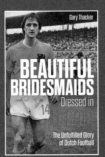

9781785318467

9781785318245

9781801500586

9781785317262

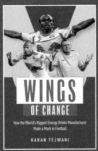

9781785317293

9781801501149

GLORIOUS
REINVENTION

GLORIOUS
REINVENTION
The Rebirth of Ajax Amsterdam

Karan Tejwani

First published by Pitch Publishing, 2022

Pitch Publishing
9 Donnington Park,
85 Birdham Road,
Chichester,
West Sussex,
PO20 7AJ
www.pitchpublishing.co.uk
info@pitchpublishing.co.uk

© 2022, Karan Tejwani

Every effort has been made to trace the copyright.
Any oversight will be rectified in future editions at the
earliest opportunity by the publisher.

All rights reserved. No part of this book may be reproduced,
sold or utilised in any form or transmitted in any form or by
any means, electronic or mechanical, including photocopying,
recording or by any information storage and retrieval system,
without prior permission in writing from the Publisher.

A CIP catalogue record is available for this book
from the British Library.

ISBN 978 1 80150 069 2

Typesetting and origination by Pitch Publishing
Printed and bound in India by Replika Press Pvt. Ltd.

CONTENTS

Acknowledgements 7

Part 1: Ajax and the Revolution 11
This Is Ajax. 13
The Wilderness Years. 24
Velvet Revolution I: All Change 49
Velvet Revolution II: Cruyff vs Van Gaal 65
Cruyff Plan, with Ruben Jongkind 76

Part 2: New People, New Success 93
The De Boer Years 95
Two Peas in a Pod 109
The Man from Apeldoorn 123
From Amsterdam to Stockholm 134
De Tukker 149
Marc Overmars's Belly Flop 163

Part 3: Ajax, Reinvented 197
Revolution 2.0 199
A Little Samba, a Little Grinta. 214
De Toekomst, with Ronald de Boer 224
For Everyone 237
Melodies Pure and True 251
Who Is Ajax? 263
Bibliography 271

ACKNOWLEDGEMENTS

AJAX'S 4-1 win over Real Madrid in 2019 is my favourite club match ever. Apart from the fans of the Spanish club, I haven't come across many people who didn't enjoy that clash. A club from outside Europe's top five leagues, one that modern football had left behind for so long, had just beaten and dominated the record European champions – a club that had won the three previous editions of the Champions League. It was a wonderful night, and their run that season was magical.

I was 19 when that match took place – not too old, and I had only watched football religiously for a few years prior. But that match, for the first time in a long time, brought back the childlike joy and excitement you get when you first watch football. From then on, it was all Ajax. I wanted them to go all the way, and, as dramatic as the semi-final was, it was sad to see them lose to Tottenham in such a heartbreaking manner. Ajax's class of 2019 will remain my favourite team for a very long time.

It wasn't unexpected, but it was a shame that team didn't get more time together. That run came as a result of years of drastic changes to fix errors of old, and adapt to 21st century football and the overall state of the game. This is what I wish to convey with *Glorious Reinvention*: how Ajax went from Champions League winners in 1995 under Louis van Gaal to years of turmoil to Champions League semi-finalists and a healthy European club under Erik ten Hag in the modern day.

As ever, no work of non-fiction is complete without the help of so many. The team at Pitch Publishing have been so great to work with for this book and my previous one, *Wings of Change*. Jane Camillin is always helpful, and Duncan Olner has done another beautiful job with the cover.

I'm so grateful to all the fans, journalists, bloggers and footballers who took time out of their schedules to help me out with this book.

In alphabetical order, they are: Amber van Lieshout, Auke Kok, Bart Sanders, Chris David, Erol Erdogan, Fabian Nagtzaam, James Webb, Jan Willem Spaans, Jelmer Jager, Joël Veltman, Jos Boesveld, Kenneth Vermeer, Leonne Stentler, Lukas Raeder, Mark Looms, Marleen Molenaar, Mateo Cassierra, Menno Pot, Menno de Galan, Pascalle Tang, Paul Groenendijk, Peter Drury, Peter McVitie, Rodney Rijsdijk, Ronald de Boer, Ruben Jongkind, Stefan Coerts, Tessel Middag, Thijs Zwagerman and Wim de Wit.

Writing this book didn't come without its challenges. My first book was written in different circumstances, albeit mostly positive ones. That was during a COVID-induced lockdown, a quieter, idler world, and a different life.

This time was different and a huge part of those different circumstances was the people I was around. I'm thankful to the very good friends and flatmates of mine at C14 who have been tremendous company throughout the process of working on this book: Caitlin, George, Josh, Lily, Oliver, Penny and TC. The biggest of hugs to them.

I also wanted to send great love to my family, who have been a constant support throughout this book and my career.

Finally, I want to thank you, the reader, for getting hold of this copy. *Glorious Reinvention* is the work of several months, one that I certainly had plenty of fun writing and researching, and I hope you enjoy reading it as much as I've enjoyed writing it.

Karan Tejwani,
November 2021.

Notes:

Throughout the book, I've used the anglicised versions of Dutch names (e.g. Cruyff, rather than Cruijff).

All competition and transfer data is correct as of November 2021 (with reference from Transfermarkt).

PART 1:

AJAX AND THE REVOLUTION

THIS IS AJAX

A brief history of the pride of Amsterdam

AJAX ARE a unique institution. A club of innovators and inspiration, revolutionaries and rebels – one that looked to the future. They've given birth to and hosted some of football's great minds and continue to influence the game around the world to this day. While Johan Cruyff, Louis van Gaal and Rinus Michels are significant to the club's modern history, Ajax's early years and British roots make them an admirable football club.

In 1894, a group of friends and students in Amsterdam, Floris Stempel, Han Dade and Carel Reeser, formed Union Football Club. That same year, they were renamed as Footh-Ball Club Ajax, with 'football' being misspelled due to an error in the registration form. The name Ajax was chosen because the trio were fond of Greek mythology as a result of history lessons and were admirers of the warrior, Ajax. The team, donning their red and white stripes, played outside Amsterdam, namely at the Willemspark and later in Nieuwer-Amstel, against fellow townspeople. In 1896, Nieuwer-Amstel became a part of Amsterdam and the city wanted to build houses where Ajax played, leaving the club with no place to play.

By 1896, interest in Ajax was dying with many of their members taking their own path following the completion of their education at Hogere Burgerschool, where they all studied. Inspired by England and the English in the country, football was becoming increasingly popular in the Netherlands, with Amsterdam a key hub – the foundation of Amsterdamsche Football Club in 1895 was a prominent example. To cope with this, the Amsterdam Football Association set up rules to provide their clubs and players with a clear structure. Stempel, however, didn't want Ajax to die and in 1900 he wrote a letter to Dade and Reeser, calling for the rebirth of a new, more professional Ajax.

Hereby, the undersigned invites you politely to grace us with your presence in one of the upper rooms of Café-Bar Oost-Indië, at number 2, Kalverstraat, on Sunday morning at 9 hours and 3 quarters, to discuss the establishment of an entirely new Football Club. – Floris Stempel's letter.

He got a positive response and on 18 March 1900 at the Café Oost-Indië in Kalverstraat, Amsterdamsche Football Club Ajax (now spelled correctly) were born. Of course, the 'entirely new' aspect of that was entirely true – an Ajax existed before. This was a more thorough version of it.

At the new Ajax, Reeser was the club secretary while Stempel was their first chairman. Ajax were one of Amsterdam's more elite clubs and most of their playing squad, like their founders, were students and had upper- or middle-class backgrounds. A registration fee was charged, which was fairly pricey at the time, and that registration had to be renewed each year. Professionalism was a must and to ensure discipline – which was a problem at the time – they introduced a strict fine system, which included penalties for not showing up to matches, walking away from matches, not carrying the right equipment and the use of inappropriate language or behaviour, amongst others.

Stempel remained chairman until 1908 and enabled the club to join the *Amsterdamsche Voetbalbond* (AVB), playing in their first official AVB league game on 29 September 1900 and winning 2-1 away at DOSB. In that first season, the club also yielded a profit of just over four guilders, which allowed them to play in their first away game outside of Amsterdam, winning 4-2 in Haarlem against a club named Oranje. Ajax were a step ahead of the rest in terms of facilities but were still playing in the second division of Dutch football for the first decade of their existence. It wasn't until the arrival of Irishman Jack Kirwan in 1910 – their first professional manager – that they went up. Until that point, Ajax wore red and white, but when they went up, they were asked to change their strip because Sparta Rotterdam, in the same division as them, had a similar shirt. Ajax chose a white shirt with a red bar in between, and that has stuck ever since.

Their stay at the top was short-lived, lasting just three seasons before they went back down. With the First World War impacting Europe, Kirwan departed. His replacement was Jack Reynolds, the Bury-born former Grimsby Town and Sheffield Wednesday player. Reynolds moved to Switzerland in 1912 to work at St Gallen and two years after that he was set to manage the German national team as they prepared for the 1916 Olympic Games. However, due to the outbreak of the war, those plans were halted. Instead, he moved to Ajax. Germany's loss was the Amsterdammers' gain as he revolutionised the club and set the foundations for eras of success.

At Ajax, Reynolds helped raise the standards of the club. He increased the number of training sessions per week from one to two, engaged in tactical discussions and worked intensely on the fitness of the team. Learning the language was important for Reynolds to improve communication as his players grasped new ideas. The team focused on fast movement, passing and the use of wingers to work on an offensive system that resembled the popular *totaalvoetbal* (total football) of decades later. Additionally, Reynolds also emphasised youth development, with youth teams across various age groups training in the same way as the first-team players. This ensured that players understood the style and could easily transition to older age groups.

Joining the club in the second division in 1915, he led Ajax to the Dutch Cup in 1917 and, following the expansion of the *Eerste Klasse* (first division), they were promoted to the top flight in the same year. A year later they won their first regional title and the season after that they were unbeaten. In 1925, however, after a fallout with the board, Reynolds left to coach rivals Blauw-Wit, but that didn't stop Ajax's British connection. Ajax recognised England's tactical nous, and that encouraged the club to continue in that vein. Harold Rose and Stanley Castle followed Reynolds, and the latter won a few regional titles, but failed on the national scene. Soon, Reynolds would make his peace with Ajax after three seasons away, and his availability persuaded the club to make the simple decision of completing his return.

With Reynolds came players like Wim Anderiesen and Piet van Reenen and, while his first task was to ensure their survival in the top flight, the 1930s were a glorious era for Ajax. The national title win in 1931 – their first in 12 years – was impressive. They scored 75 goals in 18 games in the league season and then a further 39 in 24 in the play-offs to win the championship. Four more national championships were added in that decade, as Ajax became the finest team in the country.

The increased popularity of Ajax led to an increase in demand to watch them. Until 1934, they played at the Het Houten Stadium, a ground with wooden stands, but as they attracted more fans, maintaining the stadium became difficult. With the Netherlands struggling from a financial crisis at the time, Ajax were keen to move, but were mindful of their spending. Eventually, at a cost of 300,000 guilders, which some of the players contributed to, board member and architect Daan Roodenburg designed De Meer, 100 metres away from their old stadium.

As the Second World War formed a dark cloud over Europe in the 1940s, football and sport in general flourished in the Netherlands. The country, under Nazi occupation, continued the league, but there were difficulties. Due to players being unavailable because of the war and transport for away games being tough, there were troubles, but football during wartime was still relatively undisturbed and seasons were allowed to run their course.

For Ajax, this period was challenging. Reynolds was arrested in June 1940 and sent to a camp on the North Sea as a prisoner of war as well as a hard labour camp in Poland. As the Russians advanced in Poland in 1944, Reynolds was moved once more, this time to the Belfort camp in France. That year, as part of an exchange with German prisoners, he was able to return to his home in England. Football, however, stayed close to him. His 'Technical Tips' column continued to feature in Ajax's magazine, and he even oversaw matches between prisoners and guards.

He wasn't the only *Ajacied* victim of the war. Edward Hamel, the New York-born Ajax player, was one of their greats in the 1920s, featuring 125 times. He was arrested by the Germans for his Jewish descent and eventually deported to Auschwitz, where he died in April 1943. Another Jewish Ajax player, Johnny Roeg, survived the war by going into hiding.

Ajax had built a close connection with the Jewish population in Amsterdam in the 1930s. Many of them resided in the De Meer district, and the rapport was strong. After the war, about three-quarters of the city's Jewish population had either fled the city or were trapped in ghettos. However, Ajax were always proud of the relationship and fought against any forms of antisemitism they faced in games. Hamel was an Ajax hero, and he paved the way for more Jewish players, most notably Sjaak Swaart, their record appearance maker who played for the Amsterdam club between 1956 and 1973.

Post-war, Reynolds was gone, but his legacy was eminent. He coached Rinus Michels, who would go on to become one of the most important figures in Ajax history. Before that, in the 1950s, Ajax were involved in key decisions as the Dutch game would go professional.

The Amsterdam club were losing key players to French clubs for money, something unheard of in the Netherlands. Cor van der Hart went to Olympique Lille while captain Joop Stoffelen went to Racing Paris. The KNVB knew something had to be done to stop losing their best players for transfer fees but didn't want to implement the idea of paying hefty sums. Clubs in favour of professional or semi-professional football disagreed, believing money was the way forward. They formed the *Nederlandse Beroeps Voetbal Bond*, or NBVB. Ajax, however, were uncertain of joining them. In July 1954, at their most attended board meeting, the board were against payment, but were vetoed by a majority of their members. It took until November of 1954 for the KNVB and NBVB to come together and professionalise football and two years later several regional leagues joined together to form one competition: the *Eredivisie*, and Ajax were its first champions.

That also led to their first taste of the European Cup in 1957, as they beat SC Wismut of East Germany 4-1 on aggregate before falling to Vasas Budapest of Hungary 4-0. Englishman Vic Buckingham led them to another title in 1960 but departed the same year and the decline began. Just five years later, with Buckingham at the helm again, they were nearly relegated, finishing 13th of 16 teams. However, it was in that season that things changed. The foundations were laid for Golden Ajax as Johan Cruyff made his debut in October 1964 and the Reynolds-inspired Michels took over from Buckingham as head coach in January 1965. Alongside Cruyff, the likes of Piet Keizer, Barry Hulshoff, Gerrie Mühren and Wim Suurbier all made their debuts for Ajax.

The success under Michels was quick and the rest of Europe took notice. Ajax won the league in 1966 and in December of that year they took on Liverpool at the Amsterdam Olympic Stadium with over 55,000 in attendance. With a thick fog blanket around the stadium, visibility was at bare minimum, but the game still went ahead. In *De Mistwedstrijd* (the fog match), Ajax won 5-1 and Amsterdam knew their team were ready. Dukla Prague may have eliminated them in the next round, but it was clear something good was brewing. It was just three years later that they reached the European Cup Final, losing to AC Milan, but beating the likes of Nürnberg, Fenerbahçe, Spartak Trvana and especially Benfica, who had to be put aside after three games (home, away and a play-off after the first two games were level), was a matter of pride. They wouldn't wait long for another shot at the biggest prize in Europe, and when it arrived, they couldn't stop winning.

Seeing Feyenoord become the first Dutch club to win the European Cup in 1970 must have been disheartening, but at Wembley in 1971, they showed their class. Goals from Dick van Dijk and Arie Haan led them to a 2-0 win over Panathinaikos for their first-ever European Cup. That would be Michels's crowning moment as he would leave for Barcelona after winning four league titles, three cups and one European title.

Michels was a disciplinarian, a teacher, a genius, and he inspired his Ajax team as well as many in the future with his ingenuity. Incorporating his learnings from Reynolds and using the talent at his disposal, he lifted Ajax to new heights. In David Winner's book, *Brilliant Orange: The Neurotic Genius of Dutch Football*, he described Michels's influence: 'Total Football was, among other things, a conceptual revolution based on the idea that the size of any football field was flexible and could be altered by a team playing on it. In possession, Ajax – and later the Dutch national team – aimed to make the pitch as large as possible, spreading play to the wings and seeing every run and movement as a way to increase and exploit the available space. When they lost the ball, the same thinking and techniques were used to destroy the space of their opponents.'

Replacing him was Ștefan Kovács and he carried the Ajax juggernaut forward. Given the tricky task of leading a team he hadn't built, one that had reached two European Cup finals in the previous three years, winning one, he was asked to replicate that quality. There was surprise when he got the job. Kovács himself booked a return ticket to Amsterdam from Bucharest, thinking his stay would be short-lived, but his work was exemplary. This Ajax team broke records and made history. They retained the European Cup, beating Internazionale in the final in Rotterdam no less, and in the league they lost just once. No Dutch club had ever done the treble, but Ajax did so in that year, as Den Haag were beaten for the KNVB Cup.

Without serious reinforcements or changes to the squad, the success was repeated once again in 1973, as a third successive European Cup was won. Juventus were beaten in the final, this time through a goal from Johnny Rep. After Michels left, there were doubts in that the loss of discipline in the side would affect the team and they would lose their way. Kovács, however, ensured that the players' freedom would only make them better. 'We must accept that Ajax was his opera. It was one of the greatest football has known,' Florin Halagian, the great Romanian coach, said of Kovács's side. Ajax were the most dominant club in the continent at the time and this came as a result of their constant innovation and evolution.

Johan Cruyff said in his 2016 autobiography, *My Turn*: 'In 1971, we won the European Cup for the first time, and won it the next two years as well. So, within six years Ajax had gone from being an average club to the best team in the world. And what was the secret? It was simple – it was a combination of talent, technique and discipline, which were all things that we had been working on at Ajax, even before Rinus Michels had arrived.'

It was an era of unparalleled dominance. Between 1965 and 1973, Ajax scored 793 goals across all competitions and conceded just 183. The third successive European

Cup would signal the end of this era, and the acrimonious departure of Cruyff was central to this. It was in that year that his team-mates believed Keizer would be the more suitable captain and Kovács obliged, leaving their star man furious. He would depart for Barcelona for a record six million guilders, further strengthening the *Barçajax* connection. That began a period of a few lean years at Ajax.

Three league titles at the end of the 1970s were a fine return, but European success eluded them. As football grew and clubs developed, transfers were frequent as the club started looking abroad for players. Denmark was a key talent hub and players like Tscheu La Ling, Simon Tahamata, Frank Arnesen and Wim Kieft emerged. Cruyff returned in 1981 as well and there was optimism Ajax could become the best again, but his stay was short-lived as he made a shock move to Feyenoord in 1983. Having clinched the league and cup double with Ajax that year, Cruyff, 36, was not awarded a new contract. Furious, he did the unthinkable and moved to Ajax's rivals in Rotterdam.

The common trend of domestic glory with no continental reward continued and there was also another return for Cruyff in 1985, this time as head coach. Just two years later, a European title returned too in the form of the UEFA Cup Winners' Cup, as German side Lokomotive Leipzig were put to the sword thanks to a Marco van Basten strike in Athens. This was a team of many talents: Van Basten was one, and alongside him, the likes of Frank Rijkaard, Aron Winter and Dennis Bergkamp were also coming through. However, just like the previous decade, players left after winning in Europe and, for a third time, Cruyff would depart soon after as well.

Louis van Gaal took over as head coach in 1991 and, after a difficult start where fans called for the return of Cruyff, he won them over with a distinct style – and that wasn't just restricted to performances on the pitch. Led by Wim Jonk and Bergkamp, they beat Torino in the final of the UEFA Cup in 1992, becoming only the second club to win all three of the European Cup, Cup Winners' Cup and UEFA Cup.

Once again, though, the team was dismantled, and Van Gaal would need to start afresh. Fortunately, there was a bright group coming through at Voorland, their famous academy. With a squad consisting of the De Boer brothers – Frank and Ronald – Edwin van der Sar, Edgar Davids and signings like Marc Overmars and Jari Litmanen, they reached new levels. The league was won again in 1994, while the following year, one of the greatest teams in Ajax history won the treble of league (unbeaten no less), cup and the Champions League. They also reached the final again a year later but lost to Juventus.

That year, Ajax moved to the exquisite and futuristic Amsterdam Arena, but by the end of that century most of the 1995 squad had either left the club or retired. Football was changing. The money and career progression didn't lie in the Netherlands and, in the middle of it all, Ajax were falling behind. They were the Netherlands' most successful club, but in a new era for the game, they needed change, and it wasn't easy.

THE WILDERNESS YEARS

Understanding how Ajax lost their way

IN THE 2004/05 season, Ajax's in-house couturier, Oger, designed suits with the number 1 embroidered on them to commemorate the league title they had won in the previous season. For much of the campaign, coach Ronald Koeman adorned the suit and while it was a reminder of their championship win it was far from an indicator of their present situation. That season, Ajax were struggling, and they ended the campaign losing the title to PSV Eindhoven, finishing ten points behind them, going out in the Champions League group stages and the UEFA Cup round of 32, and losing to Willem II in the semi-final of the KNVB Cup. Koeman was sacked in February 2005, and it was just one portion in the quick decline of a proud club.

Ajax were changing and the Netherlands' place in the grander European game was changing along with them. The club moved to the futuristic Amsterdam Arena in 1996 while De Toekomst, a complex of nine football pitches close to their new stadium, was their new training ground and home for their famed youth teams. After winning the Champions League in 1995 and then reaching the final the following year, they were in a good position. But matters shifted drastically over the next decade and a half and they entered an unexpected slump. That came as a result of many factors: gross mismanagement, inadequate spending, inefficient transfers, leaving their identity behind and struggling to cope with the demands of the modern game on and off the pitch.

The introduction of the Bosman rule in 1995, which meant that players could move to a club at the end of a contract without the need for the buying club to pay a fee, affected Ajax greatly. Clubs that relied on academy-nurtured or home-grown players, like Ajax, were most hit. Ajax never found the best way to respond to the ruling at the time and it became difficult to hang on to their best players. Their best quality was to develop their own, and when players left for the riches of England, Italy or Spain, Ajax struggled to respond.

Clarence Seedorf, Patrick Kluivert, Edgar Davids and Michael Reiziger, amongst others – players that were crucial to the club's Champions League success in 1995 – all left for little to no fee. Club treasurer Arie van Os called this a death blow to their football model, while general manager Martin Oldenhof calculated losses of up to €45m as a result. 'Since I had an expiring contract, I could leave Amsterdam for free thanks to the Bosman ruling in 1995. That I walked away for zero guilders was blamed by some fans, but it was Ajax's fault,' Kluivert said in his autobiography.

Ajax's 1995 squad had been dismantled by the end of the century and even coach Louis van Gaal moved on to Barcelona in 1997. To cope with the effects of the Bosman ruling, Ajax did something that was growingly popular in European football, but almost unheard of in the Netherlands: become a publicly traded club, as they agreed to sell a part of their shares on the Amsterdam Stock Exchange. In the process, they became AFC Ajax NV (*Naamloze Vennootschap* or nameless venture) and the IPO raised about €53m for the club. It was seen as a method to maintain their position amongst Europe's elite. With the money, one of the most important items on the agenda was to grow their profile abroad, and they set up soccer schools in Ghana, South Africa and Belgium.

While the IPO provided a cash boost, there was a lack of clarity of what to do with it and that set the club back. At the time, Ajax were a club back on the map after a difficult period in the late 1980s and early 1990s. They were greatly affected by the *Zwart-geldaffaire* – black money incident – in 1988 in which their former chairman, Anton Harmsen, was raided by the *Fiscale inlichtingen en opsporingsdienst* (FIOD), the Dutch tax information and investigation authorities, with regards to tax evasion in the transfers for players like Søren Lerby, Henning Jensen, Frank Arnesen and Frank Stapleton.

In 1991, Harmsen was sentenced to a fine of 175,000 guilders and a suspended prison sentence for tax fraud. It was in that period that the *Staafincident* – iron rod incident – took place. On 27 September 1989, during a match against Austria Wien, the opposing goalkeeper Franz Wohlfahrt was struck by a metal iron rod by Ajax ultras group F-side. Ajax lost the match 3-0 by default and were excluded from European competition for two years (reduced to one year after an appeal). It also made it clear that Ajax's De Meer stadium was unfit in guaranteeing safety and played a part in the construction of the Amsterdam Arena.

Rebuilding Ajax's reputation was a difficult task but Van Gaal and Ajax had a firm vision. The scandals led to the creation of a close-knit group that would oversee the daily operations at Ajax. Michael van Praag would become chairman of the supervisory board, and he was joined by treasurer Arie van Os; Uri Coronel was in charge of commercial affairs; André Kraan, a former youth player who played alongside Rinus Michels in the mid-1940s, would oversee youth affairs along with Hennie Henrichs. Each of them had a long history with Ajax.

Van Praag's father, Jaap, was the chairman of the club during the Golden Ajax era between 1964 and 1978. Michael himself started off in the game as a referee in amateur games around Amsterdam while running a very successful record store in the city. Growing up as the son of Ajax's chairman, he developed a keen friendship with their biggest star, Johan Cruyff, but in his own words, it wasn't returned in the same way: 'Johan was my best friend, but I was not Johan's best friend,' he said. From the outside looking in, people believed he was arrogant compared with others in his position in the Netherlands, but for those working with him it wasn't the case. Van Gaal certainly didn't have any problems: 'Amiable, charming, elegant, bold, straightforward,' he described him.

Van Os was a money man, working at popular Dutch company Van de Moolen & Co. before becoming the chairman of the Amsterdam Stock Exchange. Coronel, meanwhile, was the man behind helping Ajax grow. He was influential in their moves to the Amsterdam Arena and De Toekomst. Coronel was a constant feature at Ajax games and an active member of the community. Together, Van Praag, Van Os and Coronel saw the modernisation of Ajax as they entered the 21st century. Pair them with their new, ambitious head coach in Van Gaal and there was a successful synergy.

AJAX ADMINISTRATIVE STRUCTURE 1989	
Chairman	Michael van Praag
Treasurer	Arie van Os
Commercial director	Uri Coronel
Academy supervisors	André Kraan and Hennie Henrichs

A UEFA Cup win in 1992, league titles in 1994, 1995 and 1996 as well as a glorious Champions League success in 1995 with a squad of mainly home-grown players helped Ajax return to the pinnacle of European and world football. The IPO, however, set them back, which wasn't the intention. The purpose of it was to help them compete with the best again after results had faltered due to many key departures, but in the process of trying to achieve that, the club didn't have the right people to help them take that step.

Their associate clubs abroad were failing too. Apart from a few Belgian and South African talents, there weren't many notable players coming through and their branch in Ghana was shut down immediately. There was also a lack of interest in them, especially from the club's fans. 'The fans are not interested in how things are going at the subsidiaries in Africa and Belgium,' said Frank Kales, the club's former general manager between 1999 and 2000.

With the IPO and international expansion, there was also an increase in their management force and costs. By 2002, just four years after the IPO, Ajax had over 430 full-time employees at the club and their international branches, including 173 players under contract. To compare, in 1998, the year of the IPO, they had just 98 and they even managed to reach a Champions League Final two years prior to that with fewer than 100 employees at the club. With the additional influx of employees came an additional cost – the staff earned more than ever before and that left little money to be spent elsewhere. And due to the Bosman ruling, which meant that players had to be given longer contracts and Ajax had to buy more players for greater sums from abroad, the overall salary bill increased drastically too.

The IPO also led to anger amongst the club's supporters. As they became AFC Ajax NV, they were in constant communication with shareholders and, as a result, set up a 'customer service' department, which didn't go down very well. Ajax fans didn't want to be 'customers' of their club. In 2001, the department was renamed as 'supporters' affairs', but the ill feeling still remained.

From an administrative perspective, there was chopping and changing following the IPO, which did not help the stability at the club. During their tenure, the Ajax board gave themselves honorary memberships, which meant that Van Praag, Coronel, Van Os, Henrichs and Kraan became honorary members, which gave them the right to speak and influence the members' council (the council has the power to appoint, dismiss or suspend board members). Coronel, however, left his role in 1997, while Van Os was sacked, mainly due to a tax evasion case that cost Ajax €6m and him a three-day jail term. Henrichs resigned in 2000 after a disagreement over the direction the team were taking – he was disappointed over the appointment of Jan Wouters as head coach.

Coronel wasn't gone for long, having returned in 2003 when Van Praag resigned as chairman and by 2005 he would bring back Henrichs as a board member. John Jaakke would then become chairman, with Maarten Fontein becoming general manager. Fontein was an embodiment of the modern Ajax: a business mind with little experience in football operations. Prior to his move to Ajax in 2005, he worked at Unilever, the consumer goods company, where he held positions in their frozen foods department across various European countries and China.

The instability led to a stark decline at Ajax, which resulted in further financial trouble. In the 2002/03 season, they risked expulsion from European football due to their dire financial condition, having accrued a deficit of €43m over the previous three seasons. Had Financial Fair Play regulations been in place at the time, Ajax would've faced serious ramifications. In the decade since Van Gaal's departure, they had showed a positive balance over a three-year period just twice (between 2002 and 2004 and between 2003 and 2006). FFP regulations required clubs to not accrue a deficit of more than €45m over three years.

Since the IPO, Ajax had formed a host of partnerships with clubs across the world. Some yielded better results than others. The most prominent partnership was with Belgian club Germinal Beerschot of Antwerp, who were founded in 1999 as a result of a merger between Germinal Ekeren and the bankrupt Beerschot VAC. It was after the merger that Ajax took up a 30 per cent share of the club, which was later increased to 51 per cent in 2000 and then 72.5 per cent in 2001, before they sold their shares in 2003 and entered a strategic partnership. A total of eight players made the move from Antwerp to Amsterdam, with Jelle Van Damme being the first in 2001. Soon after that, the likes of Thomas Vermaelen and Toby Alderweireld would also make the switch; however, many others never even made it close to the first team. Players like Rachid Tiberkanine, Yama Sharifi and Gideon de Graaf ended up in the lower divisions of

Belgian or Dutch football or other countries like Russia or Germany. Several Ajax players who weren't ready for the first team were also loaned out to the Belgian club in order to get more game time.

Urbain Haesaert, a coach with a long history of working in Belgium, trained the talent at Germinal Beerschot in that period and he believed it was quite fruitful for Ajax. Speaking to *Sport* in 2009: 'Ajax did not take advantage of Germinal Beerschot. There was an agreement that, in exchange for a lot of money, a limited number of players could be taken: a maximum of five per year. A total of eight went in those five years (1999 to 2004). Five of the eight made it to the first team. People now conveniently say that Ajax snatched those young talents, but Germinal Beerschot didn't do anything to keep those guys either.' When asked if those players would've been successful had they stayed in Belgium, Haesaert said: 'In my opinion, they would not have broken through here (in Belgium). The belief in them was not there. Most of them were also 16 when they left. For Germinal Beerschot, it was still a bridge too far to assess their qualities at that time.' Haesaert would later join Ajax as a scout in Belgium.

The partnership wasn't appreciated by all, most notably Patrick Vanoppen, the chairman of the club (who are now known as Beerschot AC, having changed their name in 2011): 'Perhaps the club has been well off in the short term, but if you see which youngsters Ajax has taken away and how little Beerschot has received in return, you can only conclude that it was a bad thing in the long term. The collaboration with Ajax is an example of how it should not be done.'

Another important partnership was with the South African club Cape Town Spurs, who would become Ajax

Cape Town following their merger with Seven Stars in 1999. Ajax had a history with Cape Town, having purchased Benni McCarthy from Seven Stars two years prior to the merger. The partnership had substantial investment behind it, including the construction of a $1.2m training complex that included four pitches and an indoor sports arena. Poignantly, it was called *Ikamva*, which translates from Xhosa to 'The Future', similar to Amsterdam's De Toekomst. Van Praag wanted to keep the Ajax spirit in Amsterdam and abroad: 'A number of European top players have been trained at De Toekomst and formerly at Voorland. We hope to train the best players from Africa on "*Ikamva*".' He continued: 'Let the best future African talents play and train in the Ajax system. The next Benni [McCarthy] is out there somewhere. Ajax is firmly convinced that he and all future Bennis will proudly wear the red-and-white shirt.'

There were a few that made the jump from Cape Town to Amsterdam, most notably Steven Pienaar and Eyong Enoh. Ajax Cape Town also did well in their own competitions, reaching the CAF Champions League on two separate occasions. In 2020, however, after a dispute over the direction of the club, the partnership came to an end after a 21-year relationship and Ajax Cape Town became Cape Town Spurs again. Elsewhere in Africa, Ghana's Ashanti Goldfields and Ajax collaborated in a similar sense in 1999, hoping to help young players find their way to Europe. Once again, investments were made in training facilities and a stadium, but no players ever made a move to Amsterdam as the relationship ended in 2003. In America, the Ajax Orlando Prospects were founded in 2003 and also lasted four years, with the legendary Barry Hulshoff being the club's technical director at one point. Again, no players made it to Europe.

The problem at Ajax was a lack of money coming in to the club and to solve that they once again attempted to create more commercial activities locally and abroad, namely in China, where football was increasingly popular. In 2006, led by Fontein, they entered an agreement with the Chinese Football Association and capital club Beijing Guoan as well as their national broadcaster, China Central Television (CCTV). The objective of the partnership was twofold. Firstly, the agreement with the Chinese FA and Beijing Guoan was designed to help Ajax pick the best talents for their team in the Netherlands and develop the 'Ajax way' abroad in a country that loved football. Secondly, the partnership with CCTV put Ajax on television throughout the country. Millions tuned in and the club even planned a talent show for aspiring young footballers – the winner would get a chance to train with Ajax in Europe.

Excited by the prospect of this, Ajax's sponsors got on board as well and took advantage of the Chinese market for football. Adidas and Aegon signed bigger contracts with Ajax as they became the Dutch club with the most income from sponsors. While the foundations were laid in China, the departure of Fontein in April 2008 caused any internationalisation plans to be halted, and their Chinese adventure stopped prematurely. Fontein left his role after just three years in what turned out to be a crucial period in Ajax's modern history (more on that later in this chapter).

Locally, Ajax took steps by creating the Ajax Experience by the end of the 2000s – a museum dedicated to the club's history. The goal was to attract about 200,000 visitors per year. However, this didn't work out as planned. Renovation costs for where it was located were quite high and when it did open there was an estimation of just about 70 visitors per day. The museum opened in September 2011 and closed in July 2013 after a €9m loss. The plan, designed by then commercial director Henri van der Aat, didn't achieve its goal.

Fans were also initially sceptical of Ajax's move to the Amsterdam Arena. Many questioned whether it was the right thing to do or whether it had an adverse effect on the team, fans and, as a result, the club as a whole. The Arena was different. It was modern; fans were a bit further away than the more personal De Meer. There was a feeling that the Arena represented the more modern Ajax: the public limited company that now bought players from abroad, had branches in various continents and used public transport to get to the ground rather than taking a walk.

'In De Meer, Ajax was a much warmer club,' said Leo Beenhakker, Ajax's former head coach. 'After training with the first team, you went to Voorland on Saturday mornings and had a cup of coffee with Uncle Karel (former youth coach at Ajax). Whether you were (Richard) Witschge or (Aron) Winter, you went there and watched the academy players play. You knew everyone: the trainers and the parents. That's nothing to do with money or commercialism. Ajax was a club.' Upon his return to the club as technical director in 2000, he noticed the difference between De Meer and the Amsterdam Arena: 'I was mostly in my office in the Arena. I went for a sandwich at De Toekomst a few times of the week. Eighty per cent of the people more or less passed you by.'

Fans too felt the difference, having moved to the Amsterdam Arena on the back of so many successful years and then being starved of it. Coaches came and went; the atmosphere wasn't the same and the personal touch was gone. Van Praag felt the dislike of the stadium came from the lack of immediate success: 'We started playing worse when we moved to the Arena. If we had become champions immediately, there would have been nothing wrong. But now, the supporters start paying attention to the concrete, the moat and the lack of pennants. In De Meer, we had ten skyboxes. In the Arena, it's 50!' Keje Molenaar, the former Ajax player in the 1980s, disagreed, and took the side of the fans. Speaking to *NRC Handelsblad*: 'There has been more distance between players and the audience. In De Meer, you could touch the players. In the Arena, players were given the status of pop idols – that led to alienation. Even Cruyff, in his day, shook hands with supporters after training. The board failed to hold on to that atmosphere.'

There was also criticism of Ajax for their failure to use their money from the IPO to become the outright owners of the Amsterdam Arena, which was still owned by the Government of Amsterdam. The inability to do that has resulted in Ajax having to fork out a chunk of its income to its owners and, even though games sold out on most occasions, they had expenses for the stadium. Additionally, for the first few years of its history, the seats still had multiple colours, rather than the red and white that was synonymous with Ajax, which was another source of frustration and went against the fans' wishes. The Arena didn't feel homely enough.

The Arena was different, but it wasn't holding Ajax back. It was a combination of factors, and while many clubs often take time to adapt to new surroundings, the new stadium could be seen as a positive, rather than a negative, as Ajax eventually learned.

If there was something to pinpoint the team's adverse performances, it would be their shoddy recruitment. As mentioned earlier, the Bosman ruling forced Ajax to often look abroad for their talents, which was never really their forte. Combine that with the managerial merry-go-round and there's a recipe for inconsistency and insufficient results. The injection of funds from the IPO wasn't put to the best use when it came to player recruitment. Their poor spending was further highlighted by the unsatisfactory use of funds they received from player sales.

One of the main issues facing Ajax's playing personnel was the increased demand on the academy to deliver top talents. Thanks to the riches of other countries, producing one top player per generation was no longer doing Ajax any good, and while they still had the finest facilities and nurturing in the Netherlands, it wasn't sufficient enough for the long run. Clubs from other countries had the power to attract top players, leaving Ajax to choose from lesser players who could, at the very best, help them domestically but only take them so far on the continental stage. However, some of Ajax's decisions in that time were surprising, and very often they had a poorly constructed squad. While players like Zlatan Ibrahimović, Luis Suárez and Klaas-Jan Huntelaar joined and did well at the club, others such as Timothée Atouba, Teemu Tainio, Tom Soetaers, Albert Luque and Samuel Kuffour just weren't enough to take Ajax to the highest possible level.

In the ten seasons following the 1998 IPO, Ajax purchased only eight players over the fee of €5m and all of them were below €10m. The most expensive was Huntelaar from Heerenveen at a cost of €9m. While those eight combined for a total cost of €59.5m, they brought in a fair amount of income when they were sold: €80m, with Huntelaar's €27m sale to Real Madrid the most expensive. Indeed, it was the attacking players (Huntelaar, Suárez and Ibrahimović) that were most beneficial to the club. However, that money wasn't reinvested wisely, especially when they were buying Dutch talent. In that same time period and excluding Huntelaar, Ajax purchased 12 Dutch players (excluding free and loan transfers), the most expensive being Ferdi Vierklau from Spanish club Tenerife for €4.5m. The combined cost for all 12 players was €35m, but many of them were either ageing or didn't perform well at Ajax meaning they had little to no resale value. When they were sold or left the club, they only brought in €3.1m – a €31.9m loss.

The poor reinvestment was also a concern and a harsh criticism of the people calling the shots. In that period, Ajax made some significant sales: Cristian Chivu (Roma, €18m), Ibrahimović (Juventus, €16m), Wesley Sneijder (Real Madrid, €27m), Ryan Babel (Liverpool, €17m) and Rafael van der Vaart (Hamburg, €5m) were just a few. The decision-making at the top was poor. In the previous decade, Ajax were two-time Champions League finalists, but that felt a world away in the 2000s as a clear footballing vision was nowhere to be found. 'Everyone is always complaining about the Arena and the IPO. All nonsense. Ajax has thrown away millions through opportunistic short-term purchases,' former general manager Kales said in 2008.

Add in that they went away from their traditional academy philosophy and it shows exactly why Ajax were falling behind. The focus at Ajax was to develop talent, regardless of end result, but in that period winning matches seemed more important at youth level. They wanted to dominate their rivals in every age category, rather than focus on improving individuals and making them ready for the step up. While winning is an important aspect, that wasn't necessarily essential at a young age – especially not at a club like Ajax. Creating a few players for the first team and finishing in mid-table in a youth league was perhaps a greater success than winning the league and offering nothing to the senior side. Certain players were able to earn promotions to the first team, but it wasn't enough.

Cruyff wrote in his autobiography about the downfall of the Ajax way: 'As far as I could see, the root of the problem lay in the training methods at Ajax, because, as before under [Rinus] Michels, the national team were taking inspiration for how to train and how to play from the training ground at Ajax. The club was clinging to a particular vision that was ugly and outdated, and the national squad was trained in that spirit, but with little focus on improving individual talent. Too much time during training was spent working as a group, based on the club vision, with far too little emphasis on training sessions to hone particular skills. Added to which, the decline in street football of the kind I'd played as a kid meant that a young player was now working on his fundamental techniques about 10 hours a week less, and over the course of a few years, that really makes a big difference. The result was that flair players were becoming increasingly rare, which had a negative effect on how enjoyable games were for the fans.'

He continued: 'Players were also suffering from a lack of individually tailored training, not only at Ajax but also at other clubs, which explains why a lot of Dutch footballers find themselves in difficulties as soon as the plan breaks down and they're thrown back on their own resources. You see that not just in the first 11, but also in the youth teams below them, although in the youth team it doesn't surface so quickly because the play at that level is slower. It's a different story at the top. Once an opponent finds their weak spot, a lot of players haven't a clue what to do and they get found out very quickly. That was one of the reasons why neither Ajax nor Holland had been at the top of European football for so long.'

From a coaching perspective, there were problems aplenty as well. Between 1997, the year Van Gaal left for Barcelona, and 2007, Ajax appointed nine different head coaches, each with varying levels of success. Van Gaal was the only coach between the 1990s and the end of the 2000s to serve out the length of his entire contract, and he was also their most successful coach since the 1980s.

The constant changing of personnel combined with inadequate transfers and flailing results affected Ajax. A period of sustained success was unachievable: the continuity wasn't there and, more concerningly, the right framework to lay the right foundations wasn't there either. The nine coaches they had between 1997 and the end of the 2007/08 season lasted an average of 444.6 days, with the longest reign being Ronald Koeman's 1,180-day stint between December 2001 and February 2005. It was a period where they managed to win four KNVB Cups and three *Eredivisie* titles, but in Europe they struggled, going into the second round of the Champions League just once as reaching the last eight of the UEFA Cup in 1998 proved to be their best finish in that period.

Danish coach Morten Olsen was the first, joining in 1997 and having the difficult task of replicating Van Gaal's success. He did a fine job domestically, winning the league and cup double and propelling unfancied Georgian forward

Shota Arveladze to new heights, as he scored 37 goals in his debut season. Things soon fell apart in late 1998, however. Captain Danny Blind announced he would retire at the end of the 1998/99 season; the De Boer brothers, Frank and Ronald, who many believed signed 'contracts for life', announced they wanted to leave too. The club refused to let them go, but the twins were adamant, saying they could no longer work with Olsen. In December of that year, Olsen resigned: 'As those boys [the De Boers] accused me of being uninspiring, I thought I can never win this one. I should have left the moment they said they wanted to go.' The De Boers went off to Van Gaal's Barcelona in January, along with Jari Litmanen, as Ajax were crumbling in the league, falling to fifth, and exited the Champions League in the group stage.

Jan Wouters came in, but his spell was short-lived as the 1999/00 season was disastrous. Ajax finished sixth in the league that season and started an 11-month streak without an away win. A commission was hired to research what was going wrong at Ajax and they concluded that the club needed big administrative changes, including the departure of chairman Van Praag, who accepted the results, but would only leave once the club were in a more stable position. Co Adriaanse came in the following campaign, but he too lasted just over a year. His football was more Ajax-like, but the results weren't there and he was also quite feisty in the media. When Marco van Basten was suggested as a potential head coach at Ajax, Adriaanse famously said, 'A good horse doesn't make a good rider.' Eventually, he was gone after bad results, and Koeman took charge.

Under Koeman, they won the domestic double in his first six months in charge. He also slightly improved

Ajax's fortunes off the pitch, with the transfers of players like Ibrahimović and Maxwell significantly improving them. From the academy, teenagers Sneijder and Nigel de Jong were promoted while Rafael van der Vaart and John Heitinga were also involved by 2003, as another league title followed. They showed their dominance over PSV, who were in a constant fight with Ajax, and ended up winning the league with a six-point gap over their rivals.

In the summer of 2004, Van Gaal would return to Ajax after spells with Barcelona and the Netherlands national team. However, this time he would return as a technical director, and the plan was to have him working mainly with the youth set-up while Koeman and general director Arie van Eijden focused on the senior team. Chairman Jaakke was delighted with the return: 'We went carefully in appointing a new technical director. We have taken much time to fill up the vacancy in the best possible way. That the choice of Louis van Gaal was made with great unanimity vouches for the continuity of our club's strategy.' Koeman was a happy man as well: 'The arrival of Van Gaal is a very good thing for the club and me. I have the firm impression that this is the final stop for Louis van Gaal. He's said goodbye to his career as a coach.'

While the return was meant to be a fairy tale, the period was anything but. Van Gaal and the rest of the leadership didn't see eye to eye when it came to the direction the club were taking. He didn't get along well with Koeman either, believing that merely making it to the Champions League to make up the numbers was an unacceptable return for a club of Ajax's stature. 'I think a club like Ajax should be able to play in the semi-finals of the Champions League once every five years,' he said. Van Gaal also had authority over the team and the sale of Ibrahimović following the Swede's feud with Van der Vaart on international duty, where the latter accused the forward of intentionally injuring him in a match between Sweden and the Netherlands, infuriated Koeman. Van Gaal left in October 2004, four months after joining.

He was graceful in his departure statement: 'I have made my request to be relieved of my duties in the interest of Ajax. This was not motivated by the disappointing results of recent days. What matters is, among other things, a difference of view concerning technical policies and the jurisdiction of the technical director at Ajax. Everyone who knows me understands that I like clarity. Making compromises does not fit well with my character and I anticipate more differences of opinion. In light of this I have decided to clear the way. I sincerely hope that by doing that I will serve the best interests of Ajax. I would have liked to grow old at Ajax, but unfortunately, that is not to be.'

Koeman didn't stay for long after either. A day after a UEFA Cup defeat to Auxerre in February 2005, having already been eight points behind PSV in the league, he resigned. Over the next few years, the others would take advantage of Ajax's downfall. PSV would enjoy success as Ajax would have short-term managers and new technical director Martin van Geel, a former footballer who briefly played for Ajax and had a similar position at Willem II and AZ. Danny Blind and Henk ten Cate would both last for just over a year at the club, while Adrie Koster would make it to the end of the 2007/08 season on an interim basis.

AJAX HEAD COACHES AND TECHNICAL DIRECTORS 1997–2008		
Season	Head coaches	Technical directors
1997/98	Morten Olsen	-
1998/99	Morten Olsen, Jan Wouters	-
1999/00	Jan Wouters	Danny Blind (until 08/02/2000)
2000/01	Co Adriaanse	Leo Beenhakker (from 01/09/2000)
2001/02	Co Adriaanse, Ronald Koeman	Leo Beenhakker
2002/03	Ronald Koeman	Leo Beenhakker (until 31/07/2003)
2003/04	Ronald Koeman	Louis van Gaal (from 01/11/2003)
2004/05	Ronald Koeman, Danny Blind	Louis van Gaal (until 31/10/2004)
2005/06	Danny Blind	Martin van Geel (from 01/07/2005)
2006/07	Henk ten Cate	Martin van Geel
2007/08	Henk ten Cate, Adrie Koster	Martin van Geel

From a club level, though, there was a greater investigation going on to understand why Ajax had fallen so far behind not just their European rivals but their Dutch ones as well. In November 2007, Ajax appointed a commission to examine the organisation and technical policy over the past decade after a meeting of the members' council.

The committee consisted of eight members and was led by Uri Coronel. Featuring in the committee were Roger van Boxtel (a former politician of the Democrats

66 party), Daniël Dekker (Dutch radio host and chairman of Ajax supporters' group *Supportersvereniging Ajax*), Joop Krant (Ajax board member) and Arend de Roever (Dutch businessman on the members' council). They examined the organisational structure, looking at the issues facing the club off the field. Examining the technical policy, looking at problems on the pitch, in recruitment and in the academy, were Stanley Menzo (former Ajax goalkeeper and head coach of FC Volendam at the time), Theo van Duivenbode (former Ajax player) and Reinier van Dantzig (club physiotherapist).

By February 2008, with Ajax stuttering in the league and having been knocked out of both the UEFA Cup and the KNVB Cup, the 38 findings of the Coronel commission report were revealed and it pointed out their primary issues over the last decade.

From the organisational side, the report suggested that the IPO didn't benefit Ajax much: 'Ajax's stock market listing in 1998 brought no financial added value to the club apart from a one-time capital injection. The committee recommends examining how Ajax's stock market listing can be terminated. A delisting would enable Ajax to find a new balance between being a professional organisation and a football club.'

Elsewhere, the report highlighted that the club had grown distant from the fans and there was no clear connection between team and supporters as there had been in their glory years. 'There is an erosion of club love. The feeling of being a football club must return in all layers of the organisation. Although a great deal has already been done in the field of supporter policy, further improvement must be sought. This should remain a spearhead of Ajax's policy.'

Additionally, it mentioned that the increased commercialisation had made the club a soulless organisation and that reparations were quickly needed to improve that relationship between fans and club once again: 'The increased commercialisation in the past 10 years has led, on the one hand, to a distant relationship with supporters, sponsors and other stakeholders and, on the other, to insufficient attention being paid to the social cohesion that is so desirable in a club like Ajax. A structurally critical culture prevails at Ajax. This places a heavy pressure on people within the organisation.'

The technical group emphasised the need for a clearer football model which had a technical director and head coach working together along with other departments, such as scouting. The report used Van Gaal's glory years in the 1990s as an example of what it should be like. The general manager of the club should have a football background, unlike the incumbent at the time, Fontein, who had a business background. The technical director, according to the report, should have a say in all football activities and needs to be in charge of who is appointed to work with the head coach. The head coach, meanwhile, should only be in charge of his players, tactics and training.

Furthermore, the report criticised the club's short-termism, mainly pointing out that signings made by Ajax had been inadequate and had no vision of improving Ajax: 'The organisation surrounding professional football scouting is characterised by a lack of fixed procedures. Those involved in scouting do not have enough confidence in each other's judgment … It is not clear on what basis and on whose authority a number of players were recruited. Those involved give contradictory accounts. In a number of cases players were recruited without a scouting report.'

To some respite, the Coronel committee had a bit of praise for the academy and youth set-up, although the coaching side of it was lacking: 'The youth training is well organised and the youth scouting is structurally well organised. However, the quality of the youth coaches needs to be improved across the board. The scientific basis of the training methods and the monitoring of them must be expanded.'

In the aftermath of the report, there were great changes at club level. Chairman Jaakke resigned from his position and was replaced by Coronel while general manager Fontein's three-year stint came to an end in April 2008 and he was replaced by Van der Aat on an interim basis before Rik van den Boog took over full time about seven months later. Van den Boog had previously played for Ajax in their youth set-up in the 1970s, but injuries curtailed any chances of a professional career. Following that, he worked at telecommunications companies in the Netherlands including Vodafone and Orange before joining the sports sector of The Entertainment Group, an agency that represented footballers and coaches.

The summer of 2008, and that season as a whole, was crucial in Ajax's modern history, and it started with the appointment of another former player as head coach. Van Basten, who had been tipped for the job for several years, joined. His task was difficult, and the situation around him didn't help.

In the transfer window, Ajax went on their biggest spree in a bid to reach Dutch football's summit once again. The last four titles had gone to PSV, and Ajax were struggling to make a mark in Europe as well. The biggest arrival was Miralem Sulejmani from Heerenveen for a club-record €16.5m, a fee they felt was worth paying for a player who scored 14 goals and provided 14 assists across all competitions in the previous season. The club were scrutinised for this. Just a year prior, they could've signed the winger for just over €250,000 from Partizan Belgrade, but their inefficiency in the transfer market led to them paying significantly more. Sulejmani was joined by others in Van Basten's costly rebuild: Ismaïl Aissati, Oleguer and Evander Sno all followed as the outlay exceeded €30m.

The start to the campaign was tough. Two defeats in their first five league games, including a 5-2 loss to Heerenveen, and an exit from the KNVB Cup third round put Van Basten under pressure immediately. A post-Christmas slump added more problems: three defeats, including a 4-1 loss at Vitesse Arnhem, put Van Basten on the brink. They had talent like Suárez, who was leading the line and scoring goals for fun. The former Groningen player, who only joined in 2007, was loving life in Amsterdam as Ajax became *FC Suárez* – his first two seasons saw him score 50 goals in 87 appearances. However, it wasn't enough to keep Van Basten in his job and by May of 2009 he was gone, and that vicious cycle of sacking coaches continued. In came the experience of Martin Jol.

Jol was an unconventional appointment for Ajax. He hadn't ever played for or coached the club previously, and he had spent the last few years working in England with Tottenham and in Germany with Hamburg. Traditionally, his philosophy didn't match with that of Ajax, but they were able to garner some results. If Suárez was good before, he was at his best under Jol – very often, it wasn't a question of if Ajax would win; instead, it was how much they would win by. That season, Suárez bagged himself two hat-tricks, three four-goal hauls and, famously, one double hat-trick of six goals in a cup match against Wezep.

Overall, an astonishing 49-goal season made him one of Europe's most prolific forwards. Ajax were performing in the league too, going unbeaten from the start of December until the end of the season, a run that included 14 successive wins towards the end of the campaign. They didn't win the league, falling a point behind Steve McClaren's impressive Twente, but a return to the Champions League and a KNVB Cup win was sufficient reward.

There was still a level of inconvenience attached to this team. Ajax were winning and looked to be on the way up again, but this wasn't like the Ajax of old. They weren't playing in a way that was associated with Ajax and, more importantly, they weren't run like Ajax were meant to be. Jol was good, but not good enough for what Ajax desired. Something big was on the horizon.

VELVET REVOLUTION I:
ALL CHANGE
The infighting, back-stabbing, chaos and drama

IN 'CRUYFF gave form to the Netherlands', a 1997 piece by Hubert Smeets in Dutch football magazine *Hard gras*, the author highlights Johan Cruyff's importance: 'Johan Cruyff was the first player who understood that he was an artist, and the first who was able and willing to collectivise the art of sports,' he says. 'In that way he was a typical baby boomer. But he did more than only provoking the establishment by having long hair or listening to pop music or drinking too much. He was always a very family man, a religious man. He was never a Provo just willing for fun to provoke the establishment.'

Cruyff has often been rebellious in his career in football and, as Smeets put it, he wasn't just rebellious for the sake of it. From his time at Barcelona as a player, a photo of Cruyff exists that shows him in confrontation with two police officers during a match between the *Blaugrana* and Málaga. The officers entered the pitch after the Dutchman had been sent off for protesting what he believed to be several incorrect refereeing decisions. As he walked off, a story goes that he took his captain's armband off – one symbolising the flag of Catalonia – kissed it and raised it to the crowd as a sign of resistance and Cruyff's beliefs against dictator Francisco Franco. Previously, in 1973, when Cruyff announced his intention to leave Ajax, he had an offer from Real Madrid, but he refused to move to the Madrid club because he believed it represented Francoist Spain. Cruyff was different. Bold, thorough, brave and he showed it again when he returned to Barcelona as head coach.

He sold ten players from his squad in 1988, built a new one from the ground up with Barça values and history and four years later his Dream Team, a combination of foreign talent and Catalonia-nurtured academy graduates, won the club's first-ever European Cup at Wembley. 'The influence of Johan Cruyff was huge,' according to Pep Guardiola, arguably Cruyff's most ardent disciple. 'He changed the mentality of Ajax and Barcelona. His influence is not comparable. He is the most influential person in the world of football in the last 50, 60 years.' There was the football side of Cruyff and the philosophical side of Cruyff, and they both intertwined to create his legend. It was his upbringing and surroundings as a youngster that shaped him, and it gave birth to one of football's most profound figures.

In the 1960s, the birth of a leftist, anti-capitalist Provo movement changed Dutch society forever as they went from post-war conservatism to a youthful 60s revolution that would go against the norm and moral high ground that certain institutions insinuated. The Provos were rebels, opposing the higher-ups and making their voices heard. In 1965, a Provo group called the *Baastard Group* protested against the Vietnam War by sitting outside the American embassy in Amsterdam. That ended in violence, as the police tried to put an end to the demonstration. That same year, the Provos were loudest. At the wedding of Princess Beatrix to German Claus von Amsberg, a former member of *Deutsches Jungvolk* and Hitler Youth, Provo activists set off smoke bombs and distributed anti-imperialist pamphlets on the royal boat. Unable to find out who did it, the police unleashed violence on everyone present, and the ceremony was a disaster.

They were unafraid to make their voices heard, and Cruyff was the embodiment of the modern Amsterdam. As he grew as a footballer, he questioned, provoked and got desired results out of it. For the national team, he asked why footballers who represented the Netherlands weren't paid for their time and why KNVB officials were given insurance on foreign trips while players weren't. At the 1974 World Cup, as the Dutch adorned their Adidas shoes and kit with three stripes across their shoulders, Cruyff wore two and donned Puma boots.

The anti-establishment nature was also involved in the naming of his son, Jordi, who was named after the patron saint of Catalonia. Jordi was born in Amsterdam, and even though the name was banned in Spain due to the Franco dictatorship's prohibition of Catalan names (which led to Cruyff being instructed to name his son 'Jorge'), Cruyff held his own and stuck with his choice, thus making his son the first legal Jordi in Spain in decades.

In David Winner's book, *Brilliant Orange: The Neurotic Genius of Dutch Football*, the author writes about Cruyff's importance and legacy: 'It always struck me that Cruyff is not simply the best-known Dutch person alive – he's also probably the most important. How many Dutch politicians can you name? Not many, I'll bet. But Dutch footballers are

known and adored around the world – Cruyff most of all.'
This was Cruyff.

It was only standard that when Ajax were struggling in
the 21st century that Cruyff intervened. At the time, Ajax
needed change after several years of ignoring everything
that made them so great and letting others get ahead of
them. Cruyff, who had been away from the club since 1988,
stepped away from coaching in 1996, but from the comforts
of his home in Barcelona, he was still in love with football
and, more importantly, he was still in love with Ajax.

In 2010, having finished second in the *Eredivisie*, Ajax
were able to return to the Champions League for the first
time since March 2006. In the third qualifying round, they
overcame PAOK on away goals, with a 3-3 draw in Greece
helping them to the next round. Then, in the play-offs, a
2-1 win at the Amsterdam Arena over Dynamo Kyiv earned
them a 3-2 aggregate success, and they were able to qualify
for the group stages. Being a club in pot three for the draw,
they were always bound to get a tough group. The draw was
made, and Ajax were placed alongside Real Madrid, Milan
and Auxerre in Group G. There were 20 European Cups
between the three heavyweights in the group, and Auxerre
were making their first appearance in the Champions
League since 2002.

The match against Real Madrid was met with great
anticipation. It would open Ajax's Champions League
campaign that season as they would travel to the Santiago
Bernabéu on 15 September 2010. The two historical giants
were entering different eras: Ajax were sluggish for a long
time, while Real Madrid were setting the foundations for
the long run. There was great historical weight to this
game too: the two had some important clashes over the

previous decades, right from their first meeting in 1967 to the European Cup semi-finals of 1973 when the Dutch side dominated the European football scene. It was their first meeting since 1995, when the all-conquering Ajax met Real Madrid twice in the group stages and picked up two wins.

Now, though, the case was different. Just a year prior, Real Madrid had a mega summer spend, signing the likes of Cristiano Ronaldo, Kaká and Karim Benzema amongst others, while José Mourinho, the reigning Champions League holder having won the title with Inter in the 2009/10 campaign, was in the *Blancos'* dugout. Ajax were hoping to make the occasion count – Luis Suárez was their best hope and Martin Jol, who had done great work with the Uruguayan forward, wanted another starring display. Four days before the game, Ajax faced Willem II at the Amsterdam Arena in a league game, beating them 2-0 with two penalties from Suárez. It wasn't a convincing win, but it was vital as they kept their unbeaten start to the season intact and spirits were up ahead of their trip to Spain.

Then came the Champions League, and it was hardly the ideal start. Real Madrid created a few chances and after the half-hour mark, a corner met the head of Gonzalo Higuaín and went in off Vurnon Anita. The goal went down as an own goal from the Dutchman. In the second half, five chances from Real Madrid in the first ten minutes were wasted. Ronaldo, Higuaín and Ángel Di María all missed chances to double their team's lead. Mourinho was frustrated; Jol felt lucky. Fifteen minutes before the end, Mesut Özil set up Higuaín from close range to make it 2-0. The tie was done, but to many it felt over from the early minutes. Ajax were all over the place, outclassed and outperformed by their rivals – their big return to the Champions League didn't go as they hoped.

Ajax were criticised greatly for their performance. Some said it was men against boys; others pointed out the financial disparity between the two, and while there was no great surprise on paper that Real Madrid had won, there needed to be an investigation into why the gap between the two was so big and what was holding Ajax back. The Coronel commission report from two years prior made some important findings, but a lot of what they suggested hadn't been implemented or implemented properly. On 20 September, Cruyff, the Amsterdam hero, stepped up for his former club.

Over the years, Cruyff had been working with *De Telegraaf* and writing columns for them, focusing on a variety of football-related topics. In that 20 September edition of *Telesport*, Cruyff, furious about how his beloved Ajax had been run, went after the management in the hope of seeing change. Assisted by his ghostwriter Jaap de Groot, the chief of sports at the paper, Cruyff started with a criticism of the team's performance in the Spanish capital: 'Last week I saw Ajax playing against a weaker opponent [Willem II] and a stronger one [Real Madrid]. Let's not beat around the bush: this Ajax is even worse than the team from my time before Rinus Michels joined the club in 1965.'

'Two-and-a-half years ago the Coronel report came out with all kinds of conclusions and suggestions for the future. If you look at all the things that came out of that, it's one big drama,' he added. 'In the build-up, Real–Ajax was still being heralded as a unique match between two historic clubs. Two teams who have enriched international football with their playing. Ajax delivered the greatest disgrace in the club's history. After the final result, everyone was happy that it was "only" 2-0, while it could just as well have been 8-0 or 9-0. Then there was all that nonsense about boys and men, when in fact there was absolutely no age difference between the two teams. The football and Ajax's attitude just weren't up for it.'

As the column came to an end, Cruyff criticised the board, saying that the fact that Ajax were top of the league was irrelevant to him as the club had lost what had made them so great. The men calling the shots didn't impress him either – to Cruyff, they were crooks who were only at the club because they were friends with those in power. 'There's also the fact that the club has been turned into one big fifth column. That starts with the members' council, which you would expect to include specialists in every area of the club. Now it consists mostly of pals and acquaintances covering each other's backs. In turn, it's from that members' council that the board of directors is assembled, which also has a majority in the commissioners' council, which in the end appoints the directors.'

Then came the coup de grâce, the call to leave. 'So from members' council to management there's a red thread of people covering for each other, while the club sinks further and further. They've all run off with the family silver. In the interests of the club they should all leave. And then the club should start over, just as they did in 1965.' Cruyff always spoke his mind – it was in every fibre of his being to do so and when it came to the struggles of Ajax, he spoke again. This bomb hit Ajax and, more importantly, the directors like no other and set the revolution in motion. The next day, club general director and chief executive Rik van den Boog went on the defensive and said that they wouldn't strip

Cruyff of his honorary membership: 'It makes me sad, and I can hardly take him seriously anymore. But he will always remain our honorary member, because he is the one who put Ajax on the international football map.'

That was Van den Boog speaking his mind. He and Uri Coronel really couldn't take Cruyff seriously. To them, Cruyff was a legend who was unwilling to move along with modern times: football had changed, left Ajax behind but also Cruyff behind, they believed. Sandro Rosell, the newly elected president of Barcelona, had stripped Cruyff of his title as honorary president just a few months prior. At Ajax, they believed that was the reason for Cruyff's sourness. Regardless, Cruyff, in many ways, was right. To many, he was always right, and he had the backing. The board was under immediate pressure, and the results that followed didn't help.

In the following weeks, Ajax lost points against Utrecht, ADO Den Haag and Excelsior, while in the Champions League, a loss to Auxerre, a team that had a competitive and financial disadvantage against them, added salt to the wounds. In November 2010, Cruyff, through his *Telesport* columns, made more calls for action. At the time, Theo van Duivenbode, the former Ajax player who played with Cruyff in the 1970s, was a part of the Ajax members' council. First established in 1963, the members' council was a separate entity, not part of the Ajax board, that had significant power over the board. The president of the council at the time was Rob Been Jr who took charge in 2008. Van Duivenbode had a role to play in the investigation of the technical policy when the Coronel commission report was published. He left in 2010 after feeling that the suggestions made in the report were not being implemented, which further infuriated Cruyff, as he wrote in his column on 8 November.

'More than €100m has disappeared since the IPO. That is an achievement in itself. Yet the board and management continue to maintain that things are going in the right direction. That almost all recommendations in the Coronel Report have been met and that the worst is behind us,' Cruyff said. 'I heard last week that my former team-mate Theo van Duivenbode has resigned from the members' council. Theo was the only player in the members' council from the sixties and seventies. In fact, he was the only one of the 24 members [of the council] who ever made it to the first team. Van Duivenbode was responsible for the technical part of the Coronel Report – in my opinion the most important chapter for Ajax. While the board and management tell us that the report was executed perfectly, van Duivenbode left because, according to him, nothing was done with the recommendations on training, scouting, transfers and other matters. As to who is right, we don't need to discuss it here. Just look at the results, I would say.'

Exactly a week later, there was another column, and it came at an important time for Ajax. The objective of this column was to encourage former Ajax first-team players – those part of the club's glory years – to occupy the eight vacant seats (out of 24) on the club members' council. Cruyff wanted former footballers on the council to make decisions using their experience as players who have been through the system – one of his goals was a more efficient academy system and who better to lead it than the academy's successful alumni?

Cruyff's column that day started off fighting back against claims that he was trying to ruin Ajax: 'There are people who claim that I am trying to destroy Ajax. They don't understand. It's not about destroying the club; it's about preventing the club from being destroyed. That's why I took action. I don't recognise my Ajax anymore. Instead of a club that radiates warmth, it has become a club full of contradictions and opponents.' Then came the call to his former team-mates, players and colleagues to return to the club and help it for the better. 'Examine the Supervisory Board, the club's management and the members' council and everyone will understand what I mean. There is not one former first-team player in it. Not one!'

'That's why I'm making an appeal to all Ajax people to get together quickly to elect candidates for the upcoming members' council election. On 14 December, eight of the 24 members will be up for re-election, and new candidates can be registered until 30 November. A first important step can then be taken by having those seats filled with *Ajacied* like Marc Overmars, Tscheu La Ling, Edo Ophof, Peter Boeve, Keje Molenaar and others,' he said.

The names mentioned had done some fine work in their own right since retiring as footballers, as Cruyff would mention in his column. They had worked as directors elsewhere, taken clubs to greater heights and took the Ajax philosophy elsewhere to enjoy success. The next evening, Cruyff, at a 'Lucky Ajax' meeting – a select group of former Ajax players that have made over 100 appearances for the club – further emphasised his message. While the foundations of the revolution were set in previous weeks, this was the first big action. Fans took notice, and to Cruyff's joy, many of the players he called for responded positively as well. Aron Winter, Keje Molenaar, Edo Ophof, Peter Boeve, Barry Hulshoff, Ko Meijer, Dick Schoenaker and former youth coach Dirk de Groot all applied for positions on the members' council and were up for election, where about 600 Ajax members would vote. This would now become *Fluwelen Revolutie*, or the Velvet Revolution, in reference to the peaceful transition of power in former Czechoslovakia in 1989.

A few days after that column, Cruyff himself visited the Amsterdam Arena to watch Ajax take on PSV Eindhoven. Sitting alongside Sjaak Swart, his former team-mate, and Frank de Boer, his protégé, he watched a dull 0-0 encounter. That was in the build-up to another Champions League clash with Real Madrid, who were to visit the Netherlands. While Ajax were outplayed in the first game in Madrid and were lucky to lose just 2-0, in their home stadium the scoreline showed the gap between the two teams. Sloppy passing, a lack of coordination and a failure to move the ball forward with meaning led to a 4-0 home defeat – their biggest ever in Europe. Towards the end of the game, Xabi Alonso and Sergio Ramos intentionally got themselves sent off to wipe off their record ahead of Real Madrid's knockout stage campaign, adding further insult to injury for Ajax, who would end the group stage in third place.

The next week, another column from Cruyff stressed the need for changes at youth level. This column pointed out the errors in the Real Madrid game that led to Ajax conceding four goals: 'All these mistakes have nothing to do with whether someone can play football well or badly, but everything to do with the basics. And that is what training is for. It is painful to see that boys, who sometimes have been trained for ten years, do not master the basic standards. When I say that training is bad, I mean things like that. To correct this, you need people who have played at the level where these rules apply. That is not a threat to Ajax, but an action that is necessary to make the club better.' Cruyff also asked more former players to register themselves to be elected on to the members' council ahead of the registration deadline on 30 November 2010 – a day after this column was published.

With Ajax struggling on the pitch both domestically and in Europe, Jol became the first big victim of the revolution. After a 1-1 draw against NEC Nijmegen and just eight days before the members' meeting, Jol resigned and was replaced by De Boer, who had been in contact with Cruyff in recent weeks and was a known supporter of his vision. This was something Cruyff wanted – a change in coach and the entry of a person who would take Ajax closer to the football they had become synonymous with over the last few decades. While it was a big change, many issues still existed. Cruyff said to the media that it didn't solve the essential problem at the club. De Boer's tenure started off with an impressive 2-0 win against Milan which secured a Europa League spot in the knockout rounds and he earned a three-and-a-half-year contract at his former club.

After the general members' meeting on 14 December, seven of the eight former Ajax players who had made themselves available for election on to the members' council had been elected as new members. Those were Schoenaker, Boeve, De Groot, Hulshoff, Molenaar, Winter and Meijer. Ophof withdrew as a candidate because he was working closely with NEC Nijmegen and KNVB rules prevented one figure from working with two clubs. Nonetheless, this was a great victory for Cruyff and his supporters.

The turn of the year was turbulent with changes aplenty. On the pitch, Ajax were improving under De Boer but off it, matters were tumultuous. Cruyff made plenty of trips between Amsterdam and his home in Barcelona to hold talks with former players and Ajax members as he aimed to force a change at board level. The likes of Marco van Basten and Frank Rijkaard were also involved in these talks. To create better communication and more clarity in their work, Ajax formed three sounding-board groups in February 2011, following a meeting of the members' council and, later, a separate meeting between Van den Boog, Cruyff and the Ajax supervisory board that included Coronel and Cor van Eijden.

The objective of the sounding-board groups was to help Ajax in three different fields:

- The Financial Affairs Sounding Board (*Klankbordgroep Financiële Zaken*) gave the club advice on financial matters, something they needed after the inadequate use of money raised from the IPO, poor partnerships with satellite clubs abroad and wastage of funds received from transfer fees.
- The Association Affairs Sounding Board (*Klankbordgroep Verenigingszaken*) advised the club on administrative matters and included the likes of Molenaar, Coronel, Hennie Henrichs, former youth player Ruud Haarms and more.
- The Technical Affairs Sounding Board (*Klankbordgroep Technische Zaken*) was designed to advise the club on matters concerning those on the pitch, such as the direction of the youth academy and playing style. This group featured former players such as Piet Keizer, Schoenaker, Boeve and Cruyff himself.

A few weeks later, on 15 March, Cruyff, along with former several Ajax players, released a report. This was to make it clear that Ajax wouldn't succeed in the way it was working and led to the creation of a 'Technical Heart' featuring three loved Ajax sons: Wim Jonk, Dennis Bergkamp and head coach De Boer. Jonk was to be the head of scouting, Bergkamp would be the head of the academy and De Boer would continue in his position as head coach. The trio would have the freedom to hire and fire anyone from De Toekomst as well as implement their own ideas. As mentioned in the previous chapter, Cruyff wanted Ajax to prioritise individual development rather than collective results that papered over the cracks. They also wanted to ensure their youth took part in different sports such as water polo or tennis to improve understanding of competition and athleticism.

Cruyff wanted generations for the future to be taught like generations from the past. Growing up, he learned from Jany van der Veen and Rinus Michels – two of the most important figures in Ajax history and two that radiated pride for Ajax and Amsterdam. Growing up in Betondorp, not too far away from Ajax's old home of De Meer, Van der Veen spotted Cruyff at the age of ten, and nurtured him into an Ajax star. It wasn't the work on the pitch that solely led to the rise of Cruyff's legend. Off the pitch, Van der Veen was there to guide the youngster through it. Cruyff credits Van der Veen in his autobiography for teaching him the norms and values of life and teaching him how the Ajax life 'compensated for the education that I wouldn't be getting at school'. That was one of Cruyff's key goals for the revolution: more Van der Veens and more learning.

The result of the birth of the Technical Heart was a loss of jobs for many existing Ajax employees. From youth coaches to medical staff to administrative members, many had to go. The Technical Affairs Sounding Board rejected the ideas presented to them by Cruyff, Jonk and Bergkamp, which only made fans furious. Ajax supporters backed Cruyff and their former heroes until the end and at matches and outside the Amsterdam Arena chants such as 'We stand behind Cruyff' and 'Stand up if you support Johan!' were loud and clear. A members' meeting on 30 March 2011 led to the most radical change of all: the entire board and supervisory board made their positions available. They stayed in their roles until replacements were found, but it would be done: Coronel, Van den Boog and everyone who was a part of the stalling of Ajax over the past decade would be gone.

At the press conference where they announced their departure, Coronel said the decision came with the future of Ajax in mind: 'Did I give in to the pressure? No. I gave in to two things: for the sake of Ajax, this cannot continue and for the fact that at the end of the day Cruyff will always be more important than us. Cruyff is an icon of the club and for the fact that there comes a time when it becomes too much for me to continue. I don't mean that in a sentimental way, and I don't mean it in an emotional way either.' Cruyff, meanwhile, was looking forward to a future of change and eventual normalcy: 'We have a completely different vision of football and youth football. Completely different! It is totally at odds with what is happening here. What has been going on here in recent years, we think completely different about how it should be done. The moment you say, "It has to be done differently," you often need new people as well.'

They were the biggest victims of the Velvet Revolution, but the job wasn't complete. This was a significant checkpoint, not the end. There was more to come.

Smeets's 1997 column in *Hard gras* summed up Cruyff: 'All the other guys are of absolutely no importance. In industry there are no serious baby boomers; the pre-war generation still runs this country. But in sport he [Cruyff] set the tone. He made it clear that to achieve something in sport you have to combine individualism with collectivism. In a way, this was the main programme of the sixties. All the others went too far one way or the other. Collectivism ended in communism and all that kind of left-wing stuff. Many individualists lost themselves in India or Nepal. Only Johan Cruyff was able to combine both things and still is trying to combine both things.' This was Cruyff, a revolutionary.

VELVET REVOLUTION II:
CRUYFF VS VAN GAAL

The rift between two of Ajax's most famous figures

THE DEPARTURE of key figures at Ajax led to replacements coming in as this peaceful revolution would delve into bad blood. In April 2011, a committee was formed consisting of Arie van Os, Hennie Henrichs (both honorary members) and the members' council's Cees van Oevelen and Rob Been Jr to investigate the disagreements and repair the relationship between Cruyff and the club. With Cruyff in Barcelona, the committee had several meetings with the legendary former number 14 in Catalonia, but Johan Cruyff was coy, saying that he wouldn't make any public comments until the end of the Dutch season, where Ajax were on top of the league, on course to win their first league title since 2011.

With talk that Cruyff may return to the club in an official capacity for the first time since 1988, he addressed his work and future plans in another column for *Telesport* on 4 April: 'What has happened is that, for the first time in years, many great Ajax people have put their heads together to really help the club. This has resulted in a basic plan, which will have to be worked on in the future. Because theory is one thing, but practice is always another. Moreover, there has never been a plan that was without errors. Therefore, all the know-how within the club will be used regularly throughout the process.

'But we just have to start now. If we keep discussing the basic plan for too long, we will never make it before 1 July. After that, it will all have to be refined even more and involve even more specialists than has been the case so far. Because the more people who are involved, the broader the support within Ajax will be. That's why it's such a shame that the board's resignation is delaying everything. What I am already proud of is that it has been proven that footballers today can put together a plan like this. They have even come to Barcelona to discuss with specialists how things should work in practice from one organisation.' In another column about three weeks later, he asked for fans and the media to not disrupt the team in their title challenge.

In the background, however, the departing board and management created some of their own disruptions through the media. Emails from January to the end of March 2011 were leaked to the press through Dutch news outlet *Algemeen Dagblad*. The emails consisted of important details throughout the process, including specifics about the sounding-board groups, Cruyff and his agent's (Rutger Koopmans) meetings with Ajax and meetings between the board and Cruyff's crew of Wim Jonk and Dennis Bergkamp. The email of 24 March controversially detailed a meeting between Cruyff's group and Rik van den Boog. They pointed out the shortcomings at Ajax at youth level and the people judged by Cruyff, Bergkamp, Jonk and Ruben Jongkind, the former athletics trainer working closely with the group.

The email revealed that, as already well known, Cruyff thought Ajax were a 'big fucking mess' and the know-how wasn't there. Cruyff mentioned that recent results, including a Europa League exit at the hands of Spartak Moscow, were an example of how far behind Ajax had fallen. He and his group also made assessments of several Ajax employees.

Through the emails, the names and reasoning were made public:

- Jan Olde Riekerink (head of De Toekomst): 'No more finger in the pie: offer him to Cape Town or Almere [Ajax's satellite clubs]. Doesn't do what Johan wants. Not even three years ago.'

- Danny Blind (technical director): 'Doubt whether he is straightforward, no confidence and no function performed satisfactorily. Completely failed.'

In addition to that, Bergkamp, Jonk and Jongkind had assessments of their own:

- Gery Vink (head coach of Jong Ajax): 'Technical qualities are lacking.'

- Robin Pronk (head coach of Ajax U17s): 'Example of a trainer focused only on the team and results. Can't do anything right; it doesn't resonate with the players. And his father never did either.'

- Casimir Westerveld (Ajax U17s and U19s): 'Just ask the parents and fellow trainers: far too structured and fixed in a team. Not good enough.'

- Alex Geenaert (Ajax academy): 'School teacher.'

- Edmond Claus (Ajax youth goalkeeping coach): 'Less suitable as a trainer but can coordinate well. Offer an alternative.'

- Heini Otto (Ajax youth coach): 'Handles people well. Fails as trainer – can give good clinics. Offer an alternative.'

Out of the names mentioned above, only Otto and Vink remained at the club, while Westerveld left briefly in 2012 to Almere City (Ajax's satellite club) before returning two years later. Both are still contracted to Ajax. The leaked emails also revealed that Cruyff was disappointed that none of his transfer recommendations had been considered, including the signing of a new left-back, and there were also heated discussions between Bergkamp, Jonk, Jongkind and Van den Boog.

Back at Ajax, a nomination committee was set up to find ideal candidates for the vacant positions at Ajax and on the pitch, De Boer's team had ended their seven-year title drought, winning the league with a two-point lead over Twente. In June, Cruyff spoke again, making it clear that he would be willing to be a part of either the board or supervisory board, and he even invited Guus Hiddink to join him, but that invitation was rejected. Hiddink felt the politics of the matter were too much: 'I have seen the organisational model of the club and it frightened me how many commissions, councils and advisory boards Ajax has. I play some sport once a week with a couple of old friends who are involved in the club and there I witness the same pattern. They never agree; always things going on between the scenes, distrust and old feuds. They call it a big challenge, but I am 65 now and would like to enjoy the rest of my days in peace.'

Hiddink was right. Ajax were a club of too many characters, too much infighting, too much confusion and too little clarity.

It was a summer of change. Van den Boog was officially gone, Bergkamp became assistant to De Boer for the first team while Jaap Stam, Marc Overmars, Ronald de Boer and John Bosman – all former Ajax players – joined the club as coaches. The 'Technical Heart' of Bergkamp, Jonk and De Boer existed, and they had more authority, while Jongkind became head of talent development. On 25 July, the supervisory board was born, which consisted of media specialist Paul Römer, lawyer Marjan Olfers, Edgar Davids, Cruyff and company strategist Steven ten Have. On paper, it was the perfect blend between football experience and administrative outlook.

Like recent times at Ajax, the peace didn't last long. After Van den Boog's departure, the search for his replacement as general director and chief executive began. Cruyff's preference was former player Tscheu La Ling, who played for Ajax between 1975 and 1982. This choice, however, was rejected by the other four members of the supervisory board, who weren't convinced. Cruyff was impressed by his fine football career and, later, his entrepreneurship.

Although Ling retired as a millionaire, he soon went bankrupt because of bad investments and gambled his savings at casinos. Opening a fitness shop, Fitshape, in the 1990s got him back on track and branching out to dietary supplements for athletes was also beneficial. So popular was his brand that they were working across central Europe and China – even Rafael van der Vaart, the Ajax star of the 2000s, noted a better fitness record after using their products.

In addition to that, he worked in real estate across Europe, but those in eastern Europe were badly affected by the financial crisis of 2008. His earnings enabled him to purchase Slovakian club AS Trenčín in 2007 alongside fellow real estate investor Henk ter Braack. Although he had high ambitions, Ter Braack soon entered bankruptcy himself, but Ling was helped by old friends. Together, they helped the Slovakian club rise, forming links with Dutch clubs to help with their transfer activity and improving the facilities for their matchdays and training. In 2011, they won promotion to the first division of Slovakian football.

Ling kept a keen eye on proceedings at Ajax throughout the revolution. In November 2010, he made his feelings clear about Ajax at the time and Van den Boog's work. He told *De Telegraaf*: 'The Ajax culture is often denied in Amsterdam, in terms of style of play and management. In 10 years, €100m has disappeared. On the pitch you don't see Ajax playing attacking football with wingers, with home-grown players, supplemented by young, talented purchases.' He added more about the people in charge: 'The administrators and directors over the years are responsible. [They are] Passers-by often, without a football background. They all point at each other, but the current director Rik van den Boog is responsible for the fact that nothing is done with the technical recommendations from the Coronel report. The fact that Theo van Duivenbode and Stanley Menzo, the authors of the technical report [in the Coronel report], distance themselves from the current policy says it all.'

The rest of the supervisory board didn't see eye to eye with Cruyff, who was adamant on Ling. They felt he lacked the managerial experience to take the club forward and insisted on Marco van Basten as an alternative. That didn't happen due to Cruyff's resistance, and there was a stalemate again. Moving forward was impossible. In the meantime, media reports revealed Ling's previous criminal record, which included claims of bribery – that ultimately ended Ling's chances, and through a voicemail from Ten Have, he was told that he would have no chance of getting the role. One last push from Cruyff in September was unsuccessful, as he took Ling to a board meeting which ended in conflict, as Davids stormed out early. For a while, the rest of the supervisory board waited for Cruyff's next suggestion, but that never arrived.

Between July and November 2011, Ajax were without a chief executive, something unusual for a club on the Amsterdam Stock Exchange, and to help that issue, they appointed an interim management led by Martin Sturkenboom and Danny Blind. Then, a civil war began. Without Cruyff's knowledge, who was in Barcelona with his daughter, Chantal, for her birthday, the supervisory board appointed another former Ajax hero as general director: Louis van Gaal, who was set to join the club in July 2012. His contractual obligations prevented him from joining immediately as he had recently left Bayern Munich (Sturkenboom served as his interim until then).

To some, this may have been an ideal fit: Van Gaal knew what a successful Ajax was like, and now he was returning, once again. Reading more into it, though, it wasn't quite the same story. Cruyff and Van Gaal never really got along, despite both being Ajax greats. For the fans, it was like asking to choose their favourite parent. The story goes that Cruyff's dislike for van Gaal stems from a Christmas dinner when at Cruyff's Barcelona residence in 1989. During the dinner, Van Gaal received a phone call telling him a member of his family had passed away, forcing him to leave abruptly and return home to the Netherlands. According to the tale, Cruyff considered this to be rude, and didn't forgive the future Champions League-winning coach. Cruyff, however, denies this.

The feud between the two seemingly carried on throughout the 1990s. When Cruyff was asked in the middle of the decade which clubs other than Barcelona played good football, he responded with Parma and Auxerre, two clubs that had beaten Van Gaal's Ajax in European competition in recent seasons, but didn't mention Ajax. In 2000, Cruyff presented plans to the KNVB on how to rebuild after Frank Rijkaard departed as head coach. When the Dutch FA picked Van Gaal as Rijkaard's successor, he put Cruyff's plan to the side and worked on his own, focusing on how coaching should be in the future. Whatever the reasons, it was clear that the two had clashing personalities and that didn't bode well.

Cruyff was asked about his thoughts on Van Gaal's appointment in 2011, which he couldn't quite believe: 'I thought it was a joke! Later, it turned out to be true. So it's a surprise to everyone. It is, of course, completely rude.' Keje Molenaar, also working at Ajax, believed it was an axe to Cruyff's back: 'This action has set the club on fire.' Ten Have, meanwhile, said it was done for the betterment of the club, and there was no point picking sides: 'It is mainly to have Louis van Gaal on the board. He is important and necessary for Ajax at the moment. It's not about having Johan Cruyff out. It's not about a fight. It's about doing what's best for Ajax.'

Long-term Ajax sponsors weren't happy with the confusion at the club either. Ken Aerts, a spokesperson for

Adidas, said: 'We're unhappy with the unrest within the club and we're concerned about the investments we made.' Aegon's Jan Driessen had a similar message: 'This is not what we had in mind. We're extremely concerned.'

The nasty nature of the feud between Cruyff and the rest of the supervisory board took another turn when there were accusations that Cruyff made a racist comment towards Davids. According to Ten Have, Cruyff said to Davids: 'You are only on the supervisory board because you're black.' Ten Have later added: 'Edgar has been insulted and has received shocking treatment.' Davids, however, did make claims of racism towards him without mentioning Cruyff. Speaking to *Studio Voetbal*: 'Sometimes people cross the line within the supervisory board. There have even been racist comments. I don't want to go into details.'

Cruyff later explained his comments in a column: 'Ajax is a multicultural club and we have found that many talented immigrant players quit when they reach puberty. So we wanted to tackle this problem with someone from the same background, who had come through it. And that was Edgar Davids. During one of our fights I pointed that out to him. But it had nothing to do with his skin colour.' Davids, too, seemed keen on extinguishing the fire: 'I never said, and I want to emphasise that, that Johan Cruyff was a racist, despite this unfortunate remark on his part. I would also like to make clear I have deep respect for Johan Cruyff.'

It was clear to everyone that Amsterdam was only big enough for Cruyff or Van Gaal and the decision to appoint the latter only delayed progress even further. Van Gaal himself was touring Asia with his wife when the decision was made but in Amsterdam, there was a split between camp Cruyff and camp Van Gaal.

More infighting ensued as the case went to court: camp Cruyff, which consisted of Cruyff, Jongkind, Bryan Roy, Michel Kreek, Orlando Trustfull, Jonk, Bergkamp, Dean Gorré, Ronald de Boer, Stam, Overmars, Bosman, Derk de Kloet (psychologist) and Lydia Suzanne Fritz-Van der Moot (secretary of De Toekomst), against AFC Ajax NV, as they fought against the appointments of van Gaal and Blind, which they deemed to be illegal. On 12 December, the judge ruled that the appointments of van Gaal and Sturkenboom were invalid, which was appealed. That put pressure on the rest of the supervisory board, who were asked to leave after stabbing the back of Ajax's most famous son.

Just ten days later, a new board of directors was appointed. Led by chairman Hennie Henrichs, they said they would follow the philosophy of those appointed by Cruyff. In February 2012, with the appeals heard, the Amsterdam Court of Appeals also agreed the appointments of Van Gaal and Sturkenboom were not allowed, hence putting an end to that chapter and reversing all of Sturkenboom's decisions, which included giving Jonk two 'yellow cards' for his work – a third would've meant dismissal and also deciding the replacements of those that left the academy in his time at the club, amongst others.

In a column in Dutch magazine *Elf Voetbal*, Van Gaal spoke about his departure: 'People say that Ajax is now following the "Cruyff line". That's nonsense! There no more is a "Cruyff line" than there is a "Van Gaal line". There is only an Ajax line, and it has been in place for at least 25 years. I have contributed to that just as long as Cruyff has, with the difference that I was there longer. I have worked as coach at Ajax for nine years; Cruyff wasn't given that much time. The development of individual talent that is on everybody's lips now was discussed in the report that I wrote at Ajax in 2004. I would rather have become coach than general director. But I realised a director was badly needed at Ajax. Besides, I had been a director before and brought structure to the organisation. Cruyff was at Ajax now and I had no particular desire to start doing something with him. It wasn't my idea; I was asked. I'm not saying that the door is closed permanently. In my previous period at Ajax I once impulsively said, "I won't ever return until all the people who didn't lift a finger when I was fired as technical director are gone." Things are now up to Hennie Henrichs, Cruyff and their cohorts. I wish them much success! We'll see what happens.'

Cruyff was delighted with the appeal ruling, and soon the supervisory board would depart. Ten Have, who had more trouble with the courts thanks to a case lodged by Ling for libel and slander, was gone along with Römer in March; Davids and Olfers left a month later, putting an end to a board that failed to achieve much. Cruyff's work, however, would continue as Overmars and former goalkeeper Edwin van der Sar were appointed as director of football and director of marketing, respectively. Commercial director Henri van der Aat was the last of the old Ajax to leave, departing at the start of 2013. The revolution was complete.

This was a phase of disagreements, back-stabbing, appointments, sackings, quarrels in the media and plenty of people trying to input what they believed was best for Ajax. Cruyff got much of what he wanted at the end of it, but there was still work to do. The grandest drama in Dutch football at the time ended with a victory for the most-loved protagonist. However, this revolution-turned-civil war was only in the beginning. Now, the aim was to figure out how to bring Ajax back to the pinnacle of European football.

CRUYFF PLAN,
WITH RUBEN JONGKIND

Insight into Cruyff's vision,
through the eyes of his protégé

AS IS normal in a revolution, this was one of many figures and many viewpoints: some taking the side of the club's sitting board, while others supporting Johan Cruyff and his *Ajacied* vision. The need for change was clear, but the path towards it was full of landmines. The compromise required at Ajax was immense and as many of the people involved in the revolution pointed out, Ajax were a club of too many people, too many directors, too many working in the 'best interests' of the club. It was a small but highly motivated core group of people who joined Cruyff to lead the way.

One of them, Ruben Jongkind, knew where his loyalties were. He worked closely with Cruyff and the rest of the Technical Heart, which included Dennis Bergkamp, Wim Jonk and Frank de Boer. The job of those in the Technical Heart was difficult. They wanted to revamp Ajax's academy, football culture and style of play and Jongkind was heavily involved as both the co-author of the Cruyff Plan and the person crowned to be its implementation manager. I had the pleasure of speaking to him to understand his work, career, relationship with the likes of Cruyff and fixing Ajax. Jongkind starts off with an explanation of his career and how, unlike Bergkamp, Jonk and De Boer, he took the long route into football.

'Before Ajax, I worked in a high-level amateur club and in athletics,' he says. 'I was very young when I changed career because previously [before football] I was working in consultancy in organisational analysis and design, which is to help companies perform better and restructure their organisation. I love to teach, especially teaching children, and I also like sports, so it was a good decision to change career and I started working as a coach in football and athletics. I worked myself from amateur levels to working at the Ajax youth academy – that's how I started working at the club.'

Jongkind formed a keen friendship with Jonk and they bonded over the values they shared for sport and talent development. Jonk's five-year career at Ajax saw him be a part of the initial years of the Louis van Gaal era, where he won the UEFA Cup in 1992. Before that, he was at FC Volendam, his first club, and he started to build a successful career for himself from there. Later on, he had spells at clubs including Inter, PSV Eindhoven and Sheffield Wednesday. When the time came, Jonk and Jongkind were there to help Ajax.

Jongkind tells me about his relationship with Jonk: 'I met Wim Jonk and we were both using the same principles – namely, you have to observe and work with players individually to understand them and see what their needs are, and you have to tailor your training to their needs, instead of satisfying our own [coaches'] needs, which is basically to always win a match and asking players to fulfil that goal. It's not what we did. We worked in the same way, with an individual, child-centred approach.'

He adds: 'We found each other through this, and we started to note things down: how could we provide this kind of training for everyone in the academy. Because of Wim's background as an elite player and also his background in sports like tennis and golf, along with my background in organisational design and athletics, we connected. Because I was working at world level with elite athletes I started learning about individual coaching for individual sports, which is different from football because in football you have support but in elite individual sports, you are on your own, so there's a big difference in terms of mentality and performance.'

Jongkind studied the 1980s book, *Quotes of Johan*, to further understand Cruyff, his way of thinking and the Ajax way and that bolstered their working relationship. 'We both [Jonk and Jongkind] started working at the academy at the same time, in a similar role, although he was focusing on the technical or tactical side, and I was more on the physical and mental side,' Jongkind says. 'We were both doing the same things in that regard. I knew about him from before as a result of his football career and he didn't know me. We just naturally found each other because we had the same energy and same ideas. Then, we started working together as partners and became friends as well and I learned a lot about the technical and tactical elements of the game.'

As previously highlighted, the problems at Ajax at the time were plenty. Old, successful methods were forgotten, and the football club was no longer a football club – they focused more on the business side of things after their public listing on the Amsterdam Stock Exchange, when their main strength had always been to work with talent and their development. Although football and administration rules had changed – namely, the Bosman ruling – their philosophy shouldn't have been neglected.

At the academy, the approach had changed from their glory days of the 1970s and the 1990s, when they were producing players to challenge at a European level. After the Bosman ruling, some felt it no longer made sense for Ajax to develop players in the way that they did. Others had been attracted to the magic of Ajax but failed to comprehend the formula behind their impressive history and, consequently, had proven to be incapable of nurturing new elite talents. Jongkind speaks about the issues facing the academy.

'The main issue was the output. There weren't enough players coming through the academy and the players who came through were no longer "special". They lacked a key weapon or a top characteristic or skill about them that was at a world level. If you can't produce players who have that, you're doomed, because then you have to buy. And if you buy, you often make mistakes, and if you make too many mistakes, you go bankrupt, as we've seen with so many clubs. That was happening at Ajax – the club was in real trouble.'

Jongkind continues: 'In the academy there was too much focus on the team and the short-term results. The environment at the academy was not equipped to nurture talents for a Champions League level. There weren't enough training hours, not enough intensity, not a clear picture of what attacking football in the modern day should be like, and the overall environment failed to prepare the players better and earlier to shine at the higher level. Many things had to change: the idea of football, the flexibility in the academy for players who were young and needed the stimulus to grow.'

The lack of stability in the first team affected them too. Between Louis van Gaal's departure in 1997 and Frank de Boer's entry in 2010, Ajax had 13 different coaches leading them on a permanent and interim basis. There was also high turnover at youth level, which is never a good sign for any club. So, what makes the ideal Ajax coach?

'Being fearless,' Jongkind says. 'They should be able and ready to take risks, the idea that we have to score one more goal than the opponent. Willing to play players who are exceptionally creative. Thinking about having the ball, but if you don't have the ball, you have to conquer it back as soon as possible. Working with youth – the coach has to have a genuine interest in the actual products of an academy: the players. All these things are important, and, of course, we play attacking football, so the principles of our style of play are important. Play progressive football, create one-on-ones. Being an Ajax coach requires quite a specific and demanding profile.'

It must be quite a daunting task to work with Cruyff, who is arguably the most famous man in the Netherlands and arguably the most influential person in football history, especially when the task is to rebuild his beloved Ajax. However, Jongkind had the necessary capabilities: he was both a successful athletics coach and a specialist in organisational change. Cruyff valued those who could bring expertise from elsewhere and apply it to football. The two had similar values and goals and shared the ability to think outside the box, which formed a close connection very quickly.

On working with Cruyff: 'There was an immediate chemistry and connection between us. He was very goal-oriented, and he was also intuitive when we worked. When you have the same idea on things, the same philosophies and the same principles – that transcends everything. It's about thinking out of current systems and being able to think of revolutionary ideas and that was immediately there between us. I obviously knew him from before. He's one of the most famous people in the Netherlands. Arguably even in the world of football. So, in the beginning, I was a little shy but after a short while he turned out to be a very normal, social person, so it was easy for me to connect with him, and he made me feel comfortable quickly. It was not always about going forward all the time in our work; there was a very good and balanced cooperation between us.'

Jongkind also tells me about what Cruyff's demeanour was like at the time and how he handled the club constantly pushing back his plans for the future throughout the revolution: 'There was some emotion of course and there was determination. Not really frustration – just a will and energy to help the club move forward. He was very clear in his approach to the club and to the media about what needed to be done. Mostly, he was determined in a very positive way.'

The Cruyff Plan was designed to revolutionise Ajax and was the cornerstone of Ajax's Velvet Revolution. Cruyff wanted old Ajax heroes to come back and save the club, and the plan had input from them all to make sure it was sustainable, and objectives were achievable. Jongkind explains the foundations of the Cruyff Plan: 'All those issues happened, and we noted them, and then Johan Cruyff came to Ajax and said things had to change because Ajax wasn't Ajax anymore. They played different football with long balls, there were financial troubles, not many players of a world-class level were coming through the youth academy and things needed to change. And then, he invited a group of former Ajax players like [Dennis] Bergkamp, [Marco] van Basten, [Frank] Rijkaard, [Bryan] Roy, and they formed a group that made an analysis of the situation, and they needed a solution [to solve these issues].'

'Wim and I had already written our solution,' he adds. 'That was our plan. We brought that into the club in 2010. Everyone had some input and Johan asked me and Wim to go to Barcelona and present it to people from different fields to further perfect the plan. That's how the Cruyff Plan came to life. Cruyff then said that because we had conceived and written the plan, we were the best equipped to lead its execution. That's when Wim and I changed from being coaches to being managers of the academy.'

And while the cornerstone of the Velvet Revolution was the Cruyff Plan, the cornerstone of the Cruyff Plan was the revamping of the academy. Things didn't need to be results-oriented anymore: the role of academy coaches wasn't just to develop footballers who won matches, but to make sure they offered the ideal environment for players to develop and fulfil their maximum potential. The Cruyff Plan brought the focus back to the academy, away from purchases from other clubs, as those should have been targeted additions to the stable basis provided by the academy. Ajax needed to be self-sufficient again – it's what made them synonymous with the world and, more importantly, a successful footballing institution.

Amidst all the politics and back-stabbing, chopping and changing, the end goal was always the same, and it was something Cruyff and his team fought for. Jongkind speaks about what Cruyff was trying to achieve through the Cruyff Plan: 'Ajax has to play attractive football because football is played for the fans. It sounds very trivial, but it's the essence of the game. Ajax needs to play a distinctive style that everyone recognises, and it should be attractive for the fans in such a way that they can recognise Ajax by the football and not by the shirt. Secondly, the academy has to be recognised as the keystone of the club and half of the squad needs to consist of youth players. We needed to develop players who are not just *Eredivisie* level, but at a Champions League level. That talent development factory has to be based on an individual approach. As Cruyff so eloquently put it, only the first team has to win. Winning at youth level is just secondary. The primary objective is to provide the right stimulus and the right environment for each player at the right time. We have to understand the total footballer, not just by looking at the player as part of their respective age group such as U13 or U15, but by looking at the individual and what he should be in five years' time. For every player, we need a tailor-made plan to improve their skills.'

He continues: 'Third, it's about scouting. Before the Cruyff Plan, Ajax bought lots of players who were just slightly better, if not worse, than the youth players. That takes away the hope from the academy and blocks the pathway of academy players. We should only pay transfer fees for a player who is special, who very clearly fills up a gap in the team that an academy player cannot. Fourth is the performance culture. The club needs to create and maintain an open culture, where people dare to debate and even criticise someone without the fear of being fired or getting mixed up in politics. There must be a clear culture based on the principles of continuous improvement and a positive mindset. And last but not least, there has to be a deep and shared understanding that the core objective of a football club must be football and not business. Prior to the Cruyff Plan, Ajax had gradually but painfully changed towards being a more business-oriented club, rather than a football-oriented club. And in order to reverse this toxic process, we brought back a lot of former players to help change the culture back to its roots. In summary: the formula that was proven to be successful in the 1970s, combined with the addition of the requirements in modern-day elite sports. That's what the plan was all about.'

By the end of 2015, as Ajax's return to successes on the Dutch football scene were evident but further growth towards a higher international level was stagnating, there was another rift at the club, which effectively brought an end to the Cruyff Plan. Tensions had already been growing between Cruyff and his closest revolutionary allies in the academy and the people in charge of the first team, who often neglected important principles of the Cruyff Plan. When Cruyff was fighting his lung cancer in late 2015, the board took action that sapped the *Cruyffian* revolutionaries.

The rift between Cruyff, Jonk and Jongkind on one side and Bergkamp, De Boer, Edwin van der Sar and Marc Overmars on the other side led to the former group departing the club. Although this wasn't as acrimonious as previous feuds at Ajax, there was a difference in opinions on how they saw football and how to organise the club's decision-making to guarantee the faithful and sustainable execution of the Cruyff Plan. De Boer wasn't necessarily a true *Cruyffian*: there was an element of pragmatism to him and the club's desire to invest in the academy was also challenged in this period. The Cruyff Plan came to an end in 2015, as the legendary former number 14 and his disciples departed the club.

They didn't stop and wanted their vision to not just continue but also spread further globally, a wish that Cruyff had shared with them in the months before he passed away. In 2016, Jonk and Jongkind started Cruyff Football along with Johan's son, Jordi Cruyff. They aimed to share Cruyff's footballing ideas through this knowledge institute and try to impact others. On their website, they've written down what they do and base their football style on three important aspects:

- Possession: controlling possession of the ball, moving the ball quickly with few touches to destabilise the opponent's defensive structures.

- Positioning: positioning our players well on the pitch, allowing us to be economical with our effort and well organised to react quickly when we lose the ball to prevent counter-attacks and try to win the ball back in the opponent's half.

- Pressing: pressing aggressively to win the ball back as quickly as possible when we lose it. The best time to win the ball back is immediately after we lose it.

Jongkind talks me through his departure from Ajax and the creation of Cruyff Football: 'This was after we left Ajax, when Cruyff and Jonk were pushed out of the club and our team of experts stepped away in solidarity, because there were some things that we and the club didn't agree upon, and things had turned too political. When we started the plan, we needed directors. We were on the field, we were extremely busy and we had to manage the academy and implement big changes. We said that we cannot also go and work at board level, to sign off on all the decisions. Then, we said we need to find somebody who we can trust and who can do this. After a long search, we ended up with Marc Overmars in a board position.

'The idea was that he would facilitate the Technical Heart and sign off on its decisions, which was an adaptation of the traditional model of an all-powerful director of football that had clearly failed at Ajax. But gradually, Overmars changed along the way. It felt like a clash of egos, environments, an explosion of politics and that annoyed Cruyff. People were fighting for the power and status to survive and grow influence at Ajax. Then, Overmars and Bergkamp started to behave like directors, bossing over others and looking to strengthen their position. It was not how we wanted to work. They started to deviate from the plan that gave them their positions in increasingly worrying ways. So we confronted them, and we told the supervisory board to choose which direction we were going in, who would be responsible and authorised for what, and what would be the decisions the Technical Heart would take together. Jonk said that it made no sense to continue having Technical Heart meetings if this was not clarified, because this was a recipe for toxic politics. At the same time, we wanted to know if the club was ready to invest in the academy. We wanted a relatively small additional financial investment, but the board kept saying that it was too much and that there would be too many people involved. We responded by saying that in five years, they would probably make about €200m in profit, if not more, from the hugely talented fruits bared by this same academy.'

Jongkind continues: 'They refused this investment, which was one of many impediments, and it became a bit of a power struggle. Then, Cruyff said if they're not willing to execute our plan and if they push Wim Jonk out, then he would leave too, and they must no longer abuse his name. In total, we left with a group of 14 people at the end of 2015. Johan was feeling relatively well at the time despite his lung cancer, and we created Cruyff Football. As Johan put it: if Ajax doesn't want to continue in our style, there will probably be many others who do. One of his final wishes was to spread this vision of talent development around the world.

'That's how Cruyff Football was born, with our group of experts led by Wim Jonk. We teamed up with Johan, but he unfortunately died, and we then worked with his son, Jordi, between 2016 and 2019. We educated many coaches worldwide and helped clubs and national federations with their talent development systems, with an extra focus on the youngest age categories because that is the basis of all football. It was a rewarding experience. After some three years, the club where Wim started off his career in the Netherlands, FC Volendam, asked us to help them. They had finished 16th in the second division and had financial struggles, a painful decline for a traditionally strong Dutch club. After a lot of thinking, we said we'll go there and started working on a sort of "Mini Cruyff Plan".

'Wim became the head coach there, as he felt that this was the right time for him to explore what Johan had always promoted him to do: apply the vision to the first team. We're now working on the club in its totality, doing the same thing in Volendam that we did at Ajax. Of course, the context, funds and some of the specifics are different, but overall, the basic principles are the same. That's the power of the vision, that is what we do now and we are connecting the

Volendam project to our international network to increase the impact and visibility.'

As for the relationship with Overmars and Van der Sar, the personal connection has soured but there will always be a link through the work that was done by all to help get Ajax out of the situation they were in before the Cruyff Plan. The original *Cruyffian* revolutionaries cherish a sense of satisfaction and pride for the success Ajax have achieved since. As Jongkind puts it: 'Our role was to sow the seeds; others have done the harvesting.' Had Cruyff not stepped in at the right time, there was a serious chance Ajax could've spiralled even further downwards – perhaps out of the Champions League for a few years, perhaps not even challenging for domestic honours. No one can prove it as fact, but everything points towards the conclusion that this was a pivotal chapter in Ajax history and that's where Cruyff and his crew's biggest success was. For Overmars and Van der Sar, their job was to build on that, and they've done so in good fashion.

Was there always some friction in the relationship, or was it mostly positive with a sour ending? 'In the beginning, yes. The relationship was good because we were the ones that recruited them,' Jongkind says. 'We were determined to follow certain plans and they were in the board of directors advised by the supervisory board and other members of the club. There were many in those echelons who weren't keen on "giving the keys to Cruyff" – it's literally what they said. There was a lot of ignorance and ego in play. They weren't necessarily bad people, but they were influenced by club politics as well as a hunger for power and status.

'If you see what foundations were laid in those years, it's very rewarding to see what has been accomplished ten years after the very first start of the Cruyff Plan. The number of players coming through, and the quality, has been astounding. What they did well after we left was that they finally adapted the transfer policies based on what the plan said: focus on buying real and direct reinforcements. They started spending a bit more and in time this mix of home-grown talents and new signings resulted in reaching the Europa League Final with the youngest team ever and, soon after, almost winning the Champions League. Now, multiple players play at the likes of Juventus, Barcelona and so on.'

As we end our chat, I ask Jongkind a rather silly question. I knew what the response would be, but I wanted to hear it from him. 'Do you think the revolution was a success?' The answer was exactly how I expected it to be.

'Yeah, of course! What else? When we started in 2010, we said we wanted to develop Champions League winners. Nobody at the club believed it back then. No one believed Cruyff. Not even the supervisory board. They kept saying stuff like "it's impossible, you can't do that anymore". Then, Cruyff introduced one of his famous sayings: "I've never seen a bag of money score a goal." That was because they [the board] said you can't do it [play an important role in the Champions League] because other clubs are richer. We said that we will create €200m worth of players in the next five years alone. We also strongly believed that, based on our vision, we really could develop players capable to become Champions League winners and this is exactly what happened. We wanted to play attractive football, we wanted to fill the stadium, we wanted to inspire the world through helping children achieve their dreams. All of these things were written down in mission statements and posters that we handed out in 2011 and 2012. And looking back now, all of it became reality. Other people may say we were lucky, but the evidence is there – it was all written down.

'You have to look at the facts and figures: where were Ajax in 2010 compared to where they are now? How much money have they made? How many players have come through? What is the value of these players? What results are achieved? If that output was predicted by Cruyff and us and we implemented the key success factors to reach those goals and they were actually reached – it's normal that people resort to praising the philosophy. Elon Musk, for example, developed Tesla and wants to send people to Mars. Nobody will argue that it's a coincidence or luck if that vision becomes reality. Everyone will rightly say that it's the result of a philosophy and an inspirational idea. Somehow, in football, people seem to have trouble recognising and acknowledging the same patterns and that's quite strange if you think about it. Football is very results-based, and for most people it's very much a short-term story. Memories are extremely short in football; it's always the last game that counts. It's very hard for people to notice the factors for success that have influenced a club in the long term.

'Organisations who are doing the opposite – those who look at the long term like Manchester City, the Red Bull clubs, the Belgian national federation, Aspire Academy in Qatar, Athletic Club in Bilbao and FC Barcelona in the past, they worked based on a long-term vision and this brought them great success. Even in Volendam, before we started, the club was in 16th place. In our first season, we finished third and the season stopped because of COVID-19. In 2021, we reached the promotion play-offs and, unfortunately, we lost. But we have already nurtured a bunch of players who are heavily followed by big clubs. One is already sold to Feyenoord. Our efforts are visible to a growing audience of conscious football followers, but many still don't see the patterns. But we know what we are doing: the key components are in place and it's just a matter of time before the successes will follow.'

Jongkind is an articulate speaker and an interesting person to listen to. His early years in sports may not have been in football, but his insight is valuable. In his time at Ajax, which undoubtedly wasn't the all-positive story one hopes for, Jongkind undeniably played an influential part in one of the most important periods in Ajax's recent history.

PART 2:

NEW PEOPLE,
NEW SUCCESS

THE DE BOER YEARS

*How a former Ajax star helped the club
when they needed it most*

AT A mid-season training camp in Brazil in January 2013, Ajax head coach Frank de Boer spoke about wanting to take the club back amongst Europe's elite through a home-grown approach. 'Everyone has always copied Ajax's training,' he said. 'Now we want something different. And in ten years, everyone will be doing the same as Ajax. And then we will invent something new. We want to get footballers to a higher level faster, so they don't have to get used to the *Eredivisie* for two years. Players will receive individual training from a certain age. Every player needs to be treated differently.'

He then referenced American high jumper Dick Fosbury, who at the 1968 summer Olympics in Mexico City took home the gold medal with a 2.24m jump – an Olympic record. It was there that Fosbury displayed the success and potential of his new technique, the Fosbury Flop. The Oregon native's technique came as a result of difficulties in performing the straddle method, the traditional technique used in high jump where an athlete went over the high jump bar facing downwards before lifting their legs over the bar. To make things easier for himself, he created the

Fosbury Flop, where he went over the bar backwards and head first, curving his body over the bar and raising his legs up in the air at the end of the jump. His style won him the medals and left an invaluable legacy in the sport: at the 1972 Olympics in Munich, 28 out of 40 competitors used Fosbury's technique and today it's the most popular method in high jump.

De Boer's quotes reached Fosbury, who sent Ajax a message of his own, through Adidas: 'As you know, all good things come in threes, like Adidas's three stripes and Ajax's three championships in a row. Good luck, Dick Fosbury.' Amidst all the infighting at Ajax, De Boer's vision was clear. He wanted everyone to forget the misfiring Ajax of old and create his own legacy. The league title win within his first seven months at the club was the ideal start, but there was more to come as De Boer tried to take Ajax away from their troubles and remind the sport just who the club were.

While De Boer may not be remembered with the same reverence as Rinus Michels, Johan Cruyff or Louis van Gaal, his role in shaping the modern Ajax was important. He brought tranquillity to the club when it was needed most, neutrality when the club's greats were going at each other and, more importantly, he brought a sense of the Ajax vision back – something that had been missing for several years.

After taking the role in December 2010, De Boer presented himself to be a composed and reliable figure. Previously working with the youth set-up at Ajax and having played for the club for 15 years between 1984 and 1999 as both a youth and senior player, De Boer knew what was expected of him when he joined, and right from the off he impressed. A 2-0 win in their last Champions League group-stage game didn't help them on to qualification to the next round but pushed Ajax towards the Europa League. In just his second domestic league game, De Boer's Ajax beat rivals Feyenoord.

A common theme of De Boer's tenure – over five years – was that he lost key players in important moments. Within six weeks of his tenure, Luis Suárez, the club's top scorer and captain, was gone to Liverpool. While Suárez was gone, De Boer wasn't reliant on particular players, as Ajax had been under their predecessor. Instead, the former defender focused on a collective approach. There was no room for individualists – and that included Mounir Al Hamdaoui, who immediately learned. The forward was meant to be the primary talisman after Suárez's departure, but he did not often see eye to eye with De Boer.

Like Cruyff, De Boer was adamant on working with former *Ajacieden* in his backroom staff as well. Dennis Bergkamp was his right-hand man and the two had a fine relationship together as players, most evident at the 1998 World Cup where Bergkamp scored arguably the most famous goal of his career against Argentina after a long pass from De Boer. Bergkamp's role was to be the link between the academy and the first team and bounce ideas off the rest of the coaching staff. Working with them was Jaap Stam, who was the defensive coach for the first team. Additionally, Hennie Spijkerman, a former Ajax scout who was managing Ajax Cape Town in South Africa before returning to the Netherlands, worked as De Boer's assistant. Together, they aimed to restore the Ajax philosophy and ensure elements of the famed total football system still existed in the team. They wished to keep the ball moving, doing drills to ensure crisp, accurate passing in games and not just keep the ball for the sake of having it, but to dominate with it.

A crucial component to De Boer's football was keeping the ball safely at the back and allowing the forward players to take risks and use their creativity to the maximum. They would play without risk around their own half, and this helped off the ball, as they had enough players behind in case they lost possession and could retrieve the ball with ease. His side chose stability at the back rather than attacking prowess, and it was effective. In attack, the coach was willing to make a few drastic changes, such as the promotion of Siem de Jong, who was pushed further up the field and played just behind the forward. In De Boer's time at the club, he was a consistent goalscorer, and even scored twice in their tense win over Twente on the final day of the season – a win that won Ajax their first title in seven years and their 30th overall.

The 30th league title was significant. Ajax were fourth when De Boer arrived as head coach, behind Twente and PSV. Their form drastically improved after a 3-0 loss to Utrecht at the end of January, losing one, drawing two and winning 11 of their next 14. The final-day win over Twente, a dramatic 3-1 success, was relieving, and felt like Ajax's true arrival to the Amsterdam Arena, even though they had played there since 1996. Many were delighted, none more so than Cruyff, who was in the midst of creating changes at the club.

'It's a great start,' Cruyff wrote in *De Telegraaf.* 'There was a great atmosphere in the stadium to inspire the victory and all of this positivity can help open a new chapter for this proud club. Everyone knows that only a few months ago we made hard decisions on how Ajax should go forward. Frank de Boer has come in and made positive strides. Often when someone new is added you start seeing things differently and you can move forward. Since his arrival in December, Frank has handled these first steps very well. This championship should be the beginning of a long period of success for Ajax.'

'My first reaction after winning the title was that it was won with an Ajax philosophy,' De Boer added. 'It is a team full of young boys, almost all from our own youth academy, who dare to play. They have had to go through a number of ups and downs this season – but they have learned from each experience.' De Boer joined a unique group with the title success, becoming the third person after Rinus Michels and Ronald Koeman to win the *Eredivisie* as a player and head coach, and even though they lost the KNVB Cup Final to Twente, this season was a success.

Former goalkeeper Kenneth Vermeer, who played for Ajax between 1999 and 2015 (from youth level to the first team) and was a key part of their title-winning team, spoke to me about De Boer's immediate impact at the club: 'When Frank started as the head coach of the first team, I was injured and training by myself. But Frank was really clear with what he wanted from the team, what he expected from us and what he wanted to accomplish. It was really clear, following the philosophy of Ajax: building up from the back, playing good football and playing the Ajax way.'

Vermeer, now at FC Cincinnati in Major League Soccer, added: 'The season before, we were playing a 4-4-2 with Martin Jol. When Frank came back, he said he wanted to play like how Ajax are supposed to play and that's where it all started. It was a nice time overall because we were champions of the league four times in a row, and we even won the league for the first time in seven years. The players, the fans, everyone associated with Ajax were happy with winning. We had been fighting for the title for years, but we couldn't win the league in that period – we were always short on points or goal difference, so everyone was happy to win that third star (to represent their 30th league title).'

With the mood around the club still sour because of what was going on above the team, De Boer ensured some peace amongst the squad and that they didn't lose focus as they aimed to win the title for the first time in seven years. Vermeer: 'Frank has always been a very calm person. He knew what to do and the most important thing about the revolution was that everyone wanted to bring Ajax back to where they were and where they were supposed to be in terms of winning and the style of play. It all started with him. Where Ajax are at the moment has come as a result of when Frank started off as a coach.'

Over De Boer's spell at the club, there were as many as 22 players promoted from the academy to the first team and his trust in youth came in his early weeks through the promotion of talented Danish midfielder Christian Eriksen. Under Jol, Eriksen had a minimal role to play but De Boer wanted to make him a valuable member of the team. Since Eriksen, the likes of Davy Klaasen, Ricardo van Rhijn, Viktor Fischer, Anwar El Ghazi and more got chances and by the time De Boer left in 2016, academy players had made a total of 805 appearances in his tenure.

Having faith in young players, especially those who graduated through the Ajax system, was imperative to De Boer. Daley Blind benefitted massively. In his early days, he wasn't very highly regarded by several sections of the Ajax support, with many thinking he was getting a free pass due to his last name. His father Danny was a hero at the club, being a cog to the well-oiled Ajax machine that won the

Champions League in 1995, and was their second-highest appearance maker of all time, behind Sjaak Swart. De Boer worked well with two generations of the Blind family. With Danny, he formed a solid partnership and with Daley he helped him grow and become an important part of the Ajax team that won four league titles.

Blind graduated to the first team in 2008 and was sent on loan to Groningen in 2010, where he struggled to impress. Ajax considered letting him go permanently, but Jol decided he was a good depth option, putting him behind Urby Emanuelson and Vurnon Anita in the pecking order. The fans, though, were unsure. In Blind's first match for Ajax after returning from his loan spell, he was often jeered. In the 2011/12 season, De Boer often used him at left-back, turning Anita, who previously played there, into a midfielder. That season was complicated for Ajax, once falling 13 points behind league leaders PSV Eindhoven, but they managed to recover well, ending the season six points clear of second-placed Feyenoord. The second successive league title ensured De Boer followed Van Gaal's footsteps as Ajax defended their championship and he became the first person since Michels to win two successive championships as a player and coach.

In the summer of 2012, it was all change. The likes of Jan Vertonghen, Gregory van der Wiel and Anita left. This meant Blind was often used in midfield, his original position where he played as a youngster, while players such as Ricardo van Rhijn were bumped up from De Toekomst and the youth teams to the first team to replace departed players. De Boer was willing to keep the door open for those who learned the Ajax way right from when they were children, and that gave him an edge.

Vermeer highlighted the Ajax model of keeping young players ready for the first team, citing his own experiences: 'For me, I came into the first team maybe two or three years earlier and I was quite young at the time. When I joined the team, Maarten Stekelenburg was the first-choice goalkeeper and he got injured, and I had just returned from an injury of my own, so I got to play. At Ajax, it was always a mixture of players from the academy and a mixture of some older players. But, at the time, we started seeing more younger players come through and that was also a part of Ajax: at the academy, we all played the same way so the younger players could transition easily to the first team.'

The 2012/13 season was Blind's breakthrough year as Ajax claimed a third straight league title. De Boer, once again, levelled Michels and Van Gaal in claiming this feat. Considering the context, with his best players constantly leaving, it was a fine achievement to keep promoting from within and to keep winning. He followed this up again with another title in the following season, despite Eriksen and Toby Alderweireld's departures.

A year later, with the fourth championship, De Boer set a record of his own, becoming the first coach in Dutch league history to do so. Vermeer: 'We all knew what he [De Boer] wanted to do and how to make us play. His training sessions were always about possession and finishing. At one point, everything felt automatic – we were on autopilot. For a team, it was really good for us and that was how we became champions four times in a row.' While the 2013/14 season ended with the league title, they were trounced 5-1 by PEC Zwolle in the KNVB Cup Final, which stained a positive season.

Winning a title is difficult, but defending it is probably a bigger challenge, and I wanted to know the motivation for the team to ensure they remained on top. Vermeer: 'Playing in the Champions League was the main motivation. For us, it was to win the league, get into the Champions League and get into the next round. When you win the title, every team is chasing you. That's an Ajax thing. We always want to be the best. That's how I grew up and I played there for 14 or 15 years before going into the first team. That was how we all grew up. There's some pressure, but it's normal. In the academy, we're always told that nothing counts apart from the championship, so there's always pressure.'

Indeed, the Champions League is big motivation for anyone, especially for a storied club like Ajax in a football-adoring country like the Netherlands, where reaching the tail end of European competitions was a bit of a pipe dream as Europe's big five asserted their competitive and financial dominance on continental football. For De Boer, though, one of the major criticisms of his tenure will be that Ajax failed to make a mark in Europe. Some of the more famous results of De Boer's time included his first game against Milan (0-2 away win), and home successes against Manchester City (2012, 3-1) and Barcelona (2013, 2-1), but Ajax were largely insignificant in the Champions League for much of the 21st century, and that continued in the De Boer era, as apparent by the fact that they scored just 56 goals in 49 matches in his tenure.

In the 2011/12 season, they fell short in the Champions League group stages, finishing third behind Real Madrid and Lyon on goal difference in controversial circumstances after the French side's 7-1 win over Dinamo Zagreb in the last group game sparked claims of match-fixing in the Dutch media. They would fall to the Europa League, where they lost to Manchester United in the round of 32, despite claiming a 2-1 win at home. A year later, back in the Champions League, they had a difficult group with Real Madrid, Borussia Dortmund and Manchester City, and still managed to finish third with a win and draw over the English champions, eventually bowing out to Steaua Bucharest on penalties in the Europa League second round.

Once again, a year later, their luck in group-stage draws wasn't getting any better as they were given the complex task of navigating past Barcelona, Milan and Celtic. Ajax had matters in their hands as they needed a win against Milan in the final game to qualify. A first-half red card to Milan's Riccardo Montolivo gave them hope, but Ajax failed to capitalise, bowing out with memories of a famous win against Barcelona. Another Europa League defeat to the nouveau riche of Red Bull Salzburg – 6-1 on aggregate – showed Ajax where they were lacking on the European scene.

De Boer set realistic ambitions for his Ajax side. He believed a Europa League final was possible, but they were never close. The furthest they got was the round of 16 in 2015, where they lost to Dnipro Dnipropetrovsk. Many felt there were tactical discrepancies in De Boer's Ajax, making the team's football suitable for the domestic game, but not so much on the continental scene. *Voetbal International*'s Pieter Zwart analysed that. He believed De Boer's *het treintje* – little train – a way of pressing, didn't suit the European game. The term was coined by De Boer himself, and it was designed to disrupt the opposition's build-up play by having a spare man sitting in defence. The moment the opposition start building up, Ajax would have a spare man ready to break it down and begin Ajax's own attack. This, however, failed to work in Europe as rigid opposition knew what they were coming up against. Roger Schmidt's Salzburg exposed this best, and they executed their game plan perfectly.

There may be plenty of reasons for Ajax's lack of progress in Europe. In Vermeer's opinion, they didn't have much luck from their draws: 'It wasn't always a big gap. We were sometimes unlucky with who we were drawn against. We played teams like Manchester City and Real Madrid, and we played well against those teams. At the time, we beat Manchester City at home and drew away. We didn't make it to the next round, often going into the Europa League. We always wanted to qualify, but couldn't, and that was a little disappointing. Most of the time, we ended up in the Europa League, but it was the Champions League that counted for us.'

In De Boer's final two seasons, Ajax lost grip of the title, and the dramatic final-day loss in the 2015/16 season spelled the end of the coach's era. Ajax went into the last day of the season level on points with defending champions PSV but had the advantage of a better goal difference. While PSV managed to win their game against PEC Zwolle 3-1, Ajax faltered. The Amsterdam club needed to beat De Graafschap, who were already relegated, but only managed a 1-1 draw. That was one of the most heartbreaking days in Ajax's recent history, and an image of De Boer on the team bus after the game, head in hand, looking lost, exhausted and confused, summarised that event.

It was a tough ending to a fine tenure that brought back some stability at a time when Ajax needed it most, but what was his overall legacy in Amsterdam as a coach?

The successful promotion of players from De Toekomst, title wins and European downfalls are already highlighted, but there are other factors to consider. Firstly, Ajax had a significant financial advantage over the rest of their competitors domestically and playing in the Champions League every season only increased that. Before their run of winning four titles on the bounce, sides like Twente, AZ, Feyenoord and PSV were up amongst the Netherlands' best. But, since Ajax's run began, their rivals spiralled financially. Toon Gerbrands, PSV's general manager, even highlighted that Ajax could form an unbreakable dynasty in the future. At other clubs, there were big cuts made in terms of personnel and wages, while PSV, who ended Ajax's title run, were massively supported by the Eindhoven City Council.

Ajax spent the most on player salaries and, at one point, paid double of what Feyenoord were able to on personnel wages and around one and a half times more than that of PSV, who won successive championships in 2015 and 2016. De Boer had the most expensive squad in the Netherlands in that period, and his failure to create a long-standing dynasty of domestic dominance led to a feeling of underachievement. This also led to criticism of how Ajax reinvested their money. While they may have relied more frequently on players coming through the academy, very often their purchases weren't up to the mark.

One of the primary ideals of the Cruyff Plan was to stabilise their purchases and that was where De Boer fell short. The club, who often consulted De Boer on transfers, had a series of bad ones, which didn't help their situation. While players like Arkadiusz Milik, Niklas Moisander, Lasse Schöne and Jasper Cillessen did well, there were many questionable investments such as Lerin Duarte (€3m), Kolbeinn Sigþórsson (€4m), Yaya Sanogo (loan), Dimitry Bulykin (free) and more. Ajax may have invested plenty in De Boer's time, but very often it wasn't very wise in the long term, and that played a role in PSV ending their title run.

Additionally, it's worth looking at the football his teams played, which was also a key objective of the Cruyff Plan. Initially, during the title-winning years, his side dominated with a more traditional 4-3-3 or a 3-4-3 and imposed themselves on the game through their passing and high pressing. However, that dwindled in later years as possession was still a priority, but the cutting edge in front of goal was lacking. Losing creative players like Eriksen and not replacing him adequately didn't help. Ajax kept the ball, had greater possession numbers, crossed the ball into the box often but the precision was lacking. Being trained by two great coaches in Cruyff and Van Gaal in his playing days was useful, and over the course of his spell, he showed both types of football: the flowing style synonymous with Cruyff and the rigidity often displayed by Van Gaal's teams, although without the appropriate end product. At Ajax, the bar is high and beautiful football is a must, and that was lacking in several periods towards the end of De Boer's tenure.

Finally, and this is amongst De Boer's greatest successes in his initial years, he ensured neutrality at a time when the club needed it. During the Velvet Revolution and particularly in their title battle during the 2011/12 season when the feud between Cruyff and the Ajax supervisory board was at its highest, De Boer didn't add to the issues and maintained his respect for Cruyff and Van Gaal. He once said that having to pick between Cruyff and Van Gaal was like asking a parent who their favourite child was. The diplomacy he showed ensured harmony in the team and, factoring in his success, there is little doubt that he is a legend in Amsterdam not just for his playing career but for his coaching stint as well.

The issues at the club before and during his tenure were not entirely down to him, but a composed mind like De Boer's ensured they could be managed. Even after Cruyff's crew left in 2015, he remained calm.

This was De Boer and his reign as Ajax head coach. He'll go down in history as the only Ajax coach to win four successive championships and the man that put a troubled club back on the map, but there were still loose ends that needed tying, and that was something he couldn't provide. While his career after Ajax may not have gone as planned, failing to achieve much of note in England, Italy, the United States of America and with the Dutch national team, his spell at Ajax showed his qualities. He brought back the Ajax feeling that was lost for several years before him, made the academy important again, won trophies and while he may not be thought of in the same regard as many of his predecessors and successors, his time at the club was fundamental to them becoming a force once again.

TWO PEAS IN A POD

The rise of Edwin van der Sar and Marc Overmars

BARCELONA, SPAIN. Wim de Wit and Edwin van der Sar from the Johan Cruyff Institute are together touring the city, when the former goalkeeper tells De Wit what a good mentor he is and how much he appreciated his support over the years. De Wit, the founder of the institute and a lecturer in sports marketing and leadership, and Van der Sar, an ambitious student looking to make a mark on the business side of the game having done so well in net for nearly two decades for a host of top European clubs, had a positive relationship.

'Edwin was always there for all my lectures,' De Wit, now retired, tells me about his experiences teaching Van der Sar. 'In all of them, he was a very serious student. I know that his colleagues were happy to have him there. I taught him sports marketing and a little bit of leadership. He was also a very good influence on many of the other students, which also has a little bit to do with his name. He was really hard-working and keen on understanding the marketing, management and leadership concepts. So, I can't complain about him at all. For me, he was a very good student.'

The Johan Cruyff Institute is an elite finishing school for those aspiring to work in sports management, marketing, business and coaching with four campuses around the world in Amsterdam, Barcelona, Mexico City and Lima. First opened in 2002 in Barcelona, its foundations were laid three years prior in Amsterdam with the Johan Cruyff Academy, and Cruyff himself believed that those who were passionate about sport in their lives were best equipped to lead sporting organisations. Like every principle of his, Cruyff wanted things to be sports-oriented, not money-motivated, and the institute was the perfect embodiment of that. Over the years, several high-profile athletes were educated at the institute including Mexican goalkeeper Guillermo Ochoa, Dutch Paralympic sprinter Marlou van Rhijn, Spanish water polo player Jennifer Pareja and more.

De Wit himself worked with Cruyff to set up the institute. A former Ajax player, he played with Cruyff in the Amsterdam club's youth teams, and they had a close relationship. Nowadays, he counsels a few students, but when he first started off in education, he set up the framework for the Johan Cruyff Institute around the world and even taught various courses. The teachings of the institute are closely aligned with Ajax values: ensuring students learn from experience, embracing modernity, maintaining a positive team spirit and keeping their community in mind.

For many of their students who previously had some involvement with Ajax when they were younger, the goal is to work at Ajax, and for Van der Sar, it was no different. 'His ambition was to work at Ajax,' De Wit says about Van der Sar's targets. 'It was his first objective. Because of his time playing in England, he wanted to be in a directorial position at Ajax, so he was very clear in what he wanted to do.'

Indeed, it was the spell at Manchester United that encouraged him to go into working in an administrative position. When footballers retire, many of them go into coaching or being ambassadors for clubs, but for Van der Sar it was different. At Manchester United, the embodiment of hyper-capitalism in football during his time there, Van der Sar watched figures boost the club's popularity. Former chief executive David Gill was an inspiration for the goalkeeper. He watched Gill in action during United's preseason tours in the United States and Far East and picked up from it. Straight after the last game of his career – the Red Devils' Champions League Final defeat against Barcelona in 2011 – he enrolled to the Johan Cruyff Institute, declining offers from Manchester United to become a foreign ambassador, a role which would have earned him fair money and been far less stressful.

Van der Sar made his official return to Ajax in November 2012 – 13 years after he left as a player. At the height of the Velvet Revolution, he joined to become the club's first-ever marketing director, effectively replacing the commercial director, and had two major responsibilities: first, he had to help find the club a new principal sponsor, and second, he had to expand the club's reach in China, a country with plenty of interest in Ajax, but no real connection due to Ajax's lack of visibility there. He was to be helped by Michael Kinsbergen, the club's new general manager, as well as Menno Geelen, the head of commerce, both of whom would also have similar responsibilities and help mould Van der Sar in football administration. Some were sceptical of his return, calling out the nepotism, while others believed he needed more experience at a lower level, especially considering the risk Ajax were taking having lost so much money in recent times. However, Van der Sar felt ready.

Within a year and a half of his appointment, Van der Sar enjoyed great success in his role. The major coup was his deals with Chinese companies. Cheng Shin Tire (CST), the Taiwanese company that specialised in tyres for cars and bicycles, became an official sponsor in 2013. In May 2014, Ajax and technology company Huawei entered a five-year partnership. Huawei had a long interest in football, having previously worked with Atlético Madrid and Borussia Dortmund, and while there was talk that they would become Ajax's main sponsor, nothing of that sort materialised. Instead, they were merely partners and Huawei set up the largest open wireless LAN infrastructure in the Netherlands in the Amsterdam Arena in 2015. Additionally, there was also a partnership with Sengled, the lighting company, who were also now a sponsor.

The big catch in China, though, was *Football Dream*, a talent show for aspiring Chinese footballers in 2013. The show was broadcast for 13 Saturday nights, attracting over 400 million viewers on Chinese national television. This was seen as an essential event to boost Ajax's standing in China. In 2013, Van der Sar, along with ex-Ajax players Ronald de Boer and Aron Winter, visited the country to promote the event and at the start of the 2013/14 season 17 participants from the programme visited Amsterdam and had a training session at De Toekomst, as well as a meeting with the first-team coaching staff including Frank de Boer and Dennis Bergkamp.

'The *Football Dream* television format fits in perfectly with Ajax's core activities,' Van der Sar said. 'After all, training young football talents is our lifeline. In addition, China is one of the largest and most important countries in the world.' Ajax management of old – namely that led by Maarten Fontein – wanted to explore China as well, but none were as successful as the team led by Van der Sar. In China, Ajax didn't have the same popularity as the top Premier League and La Liga clubs, but through an intensive approach, the Dutch giants were looking to build their base and Van der Sar was at the forefront of their efforts. This was a different task to guarding the nets, but it was a task Van der Sar thoroughly enjoyed.

Van der Sar was developing a strong association with Chinese companies and the country as a whole, so much so that when President Xi Jingping visited Amsterdam in 2014, the former goalkeeper was invited to a meal with the Dutch royal family including King Willem-Alexander and Queen Máxima and the Chinese head of state. The King and Jingping were both avid football fans and with Van der Sar they discussed the growth of the sport in China. About a year later, there was also a partnership with LeSports, the video-streaming company that broadcasted Ajax TV across China on the internet, becoming Ajax's fourth Chinese sponsor since Van der Sar joined. The purpose was to show highlights of Ajax's fixtures throughout the season in a three-year partnership while also hosting other Ajax-related content, such as documentaries on previous great Ajax teams.

On the sponsorship front, he enjoyed another big win. Sponsorships, especially principal sponsors who appear on the front of teams' shirts, are important to Dutch clubs. Unlike Europe's big five leagues, TV coverage doesn't bring Dutch clubs as much money and with the deal with Aegon, the insurance company who had partnered with Ajax since 2008, quickly running out, Ajax needed a new deal quickly. In November 2014, after going through a list of 80 companies along with Kinsbergen and Geelen, Ajax struck a cooperation with cable operator Ziggo. The four-and-a-half-year deal with Ziggo was going to bring in €8m annually with €2m in variable payments based on the team's performances. 'This feels like a prize,' Van der Sar said upon securing the club's fourth first-team shirt sponsors, after TDK, ABN Amro and Aegon. To add to it, these sponsorship deals were also concluded without the need for a supporting agency, which would usually take between 10 and 15 per cent of the cut, making it a successful negotiation altogether.

It didn't stop there. In his time at Manchester United, Van der Sar recognised how the club had separate sponsors for their training gear and he wanted something similar at Ajax. In their deal with Ziggo, the Dutch giants retained the rights to have separate sponsors for their youth and women's teams as well as their academy, De Toekomst. Those sponsorship rights were sold to ABN Amro for €2.5m per year and €300,000 in variable payments. In total, they had the chance to earn €10.5m every year from shirt sponsorships, with variable payments potentially taking it up to €12.8m, bigger than any previous deal they had. 'While Aegon was still our main kit sponsor, we noticed that we weren't capitalising on all the press the Ajax players were generating from their training sessions,' Van der Sar said to *Marketing Week*. 'So, much like the United model, we introduced a separate training kit sponsor.'

It wasn't just foreign and main sponsors Ajax were looking at. There were extensions with long-standing ones and new deals that helped the club's budget. In his time, extensions with companies such as couturier Oger, who had been with Ajax for over two decades, Accor Hotels, Hublot and more. All of this led to his promotion to chief executive in 2016, a role held by Kinsbergen until 2015. Van der Sar was offered the role in the previous year, but felt he wasn't ready for the jump. Instead, it was given to Dolf Collee for a year before Van der Sar jumped in. The job he did was impressive, and he wasn't alone in it. Around him were people of similar stature – those who knew and understood Ajax – and together they wanted to help the club return to the very top once again.

'Success is made together with other people,' De Wit says to me on Van der Sar's work. 'He had people around him who could help him in his initial years. His status [as a former goalkeeper], at that moment, was very important for people to believe in him.' Indeed, he wasn't alone. Having the experience of Kinsbergen and Geelen around him was important and they shared their knowledge to help Van der Sar become even better. Kinsbergen once highlighted the 2014 KNVB Cup Final defeat against PEC Zwolle as the point where he noted Van der Sar's leadership qualities. With Ajax leading 1-0, the game was disrupted by fans throwing fireworks on to the pitch, leading to Van der Sar asking the supporters to 'stop with their shit'. Unfortunately, Ajax would lose 4-1, but it left a mark.

Also at the club was an air of change on the footballing front – the main front. Marc Overmars led that. Right from his playing days, Overmars had a shrewd business side, and he combined that well with his football. The winger started off at Go Ahead Eagles before joining Ajax just prior to the peak of the Louis van Gaal era, playing in and winning the Champions League in 1995. He then moved to England with Arsenal and Spain with Barcelona, but persistent knee troubles forced him to end his career relatively early in 2004, at the age of 31. As a player, Overmars maintained a quiet personality, rarely talking about his business ventures, but he was smart about it and had good people around him to lead him in the right direction. It wasn't until 2002 and his appearance in the *Quote 500* list that people took notice of his non-football activities.

Created by *Quote*, a Dutch business and finance magazine, the *Quote 500* list ranks the 500 richest people in the Netherlands. In 2002, Overmars was ranked at 462, with an estimated wealth of €38m, becoming the youngest millionaire on that list at the age of 29. Working with his father, Ben, and his brother, Edwin, Marc and his family made the Overmars business empire big. What started as something small with the purchase of a bicycle shop in the 1990s became a multimillion Euro dynasty and it came as a result of smart planning, timing and execution. 'At first, we financed almost everything with Marc's money, but that was unsustainable,' Ben Overmars said in an interview with *de Volkskrant* in 2005. 'Now the division is often: 60 per cent debt, 40 per cent equity. The real estate guys do everything with borrowed money.'

Soon after the purchase of the bicycle shop, they expanded into different fields and industries. They added a sports chain, Time Out by Marc Overmars, and also De Middenstip, a restaurant in Epe, where Overmars was born. Additionally, there was also Overmars Vastgoed BV, a property management company, and Overmars Classic Cars, a company that rented out fancy, high-end vehicles for big events and weddings, which was born out of the idea of Overmars refurbishing his first purchased car – a Jaguar – when he was playing at Willem II in the early 1990s. The family moved into real estate in the late 1990s and soon had 50 properties including holiday homes, bungalows and company spaces. There was a mix of many interests, and Overmars had a big say in how things were done, believing that it would benefit him later in life.

In 2005, with his personal wealth exceeding €44m, he dipped into football, making a €100,000 investment in his boyhood club, Go Ahead Eagles, where he also joined the board and became a commissioner for football affairs on a voluntary basis, using his football expertise to better the club. At the time, Go Ahead Eagles had a debt of around €2m and gloomy prospects for the future. In time, using his skill and knowledge from people around him, they became one of the healthier teams in Dutch football, although promotion to the *Eredivisie* was never achieved in his time.

Overmars was often involved in the financial side of things, including transfers, and his negotiation skills gained praise during his time at the club: 'He never did crazy things, always thought carefully and made well-considered decisions,' Edwin Mulder told NOS in 2019. Mulder was the club's former chairman who worked with Overmars for five years at Go Ahead Eagles. 'That negotiating is a bit ingrained. He thinks it is a sport: to see if you can reach the pain threshold, whether it is about buying or selling. That is very good for a club. He did that in a pleasant way. It's never been the case that we had terrible fights with clubs or agents. But he did try to get the most out of it in his own way. There is no one in the football world who hates Marc.'

In their rise, Overmars had a part to play as well. During Jaap Stam's testimonial in Zwolle between Ajax and a team comprised of Stam's former team-mates, Overmars was on the latter and shone, giving Romanian international right-back George Ogăraru plenty of problems and even scoring.

Unusual in a testimonial, there were plenty watching and impressed, and he received offers from Germany and the Netherlands to revive his playing career.

He refused every approach, except the one from Go Ahead Eagles, and made his return to the second-division team in the 2008/09 season. After 1,545 days out of the game, his second debut for the club was against Fortuna Sittard at home as the 4,600 fans at the ground rose for a rapturous applause. The season was difficult: Overmars failed to score and sporadically played due to his injuries, but it was a heroic return. In his final home match against TOP Oss, Overmars came on as a substitute but, within minutes, tumbled and was injured again. The stretchers were prepared, but a determined Overmars would hobble off the pitch. 'I'm not going to get off the field on a stretcher in my last game,' he said. The relationship with the club didn't end there, though. He would go back to his administrative role and lead from above.

Like his playing career, his administrative career went from Go Ahead Eagles to Ajax as well, joining the Amsterdammers first as a part-time youth coach in 2011 and then as their director of football. Johan Cruyff was an advocate of the return, praising Overmars for his work off the pitch and at Go Ahead Eagles, and he was delighted to see him back permanently in the summer of 2012.

Speaking to the Ajax website, head coach De Boer was happy to see his former team-mates (including Van der Sar) return: 'Of course I have known Marc [Overmars] and Edwin [Van der Sar] for years. We have been through a lot. After our careers we have always kept in touch. It's great that so many years later we now belong to the Ajax family again. A lot of former players were already walking around at De Toekomst, but mostly in the position of trainer. That is different from the role that Dennis Bergkamp, Wim Jonk and I (within the Technical Heart) have within the club.' Ajax, though, was a different task from Go Ahead Eagles. This was a publicly listed club trying to get back on the map.

Overmars's early work caught the eye. Cruyff, in his columns for *De Telegraaf* wished for Overmars to clean up Ajax first and then start building while reducing the influence of money-hungry agents at the club, and the former winger obliged. In his first transfer window, 15 players departed. While some of these players such as Jan Vertonghen and Gregory van der Wiel were important to the first team, the allure of other leagues was too hard to resist. Others had slim prospects and were hardly going to be used – they had to go. Overmars also backed out of complex and expensive negotiations with Heerenveen and agent Mino Raiola over the transfer of Oussama Assaidi, who moved to Liverpool instead.

However, while Ajax were making sales and cutting down costs in their squad, Overmars was often criticised for his frugal nature. During his time as a player at Ajax, he earned the nickname *Marc Netto* – Marc Net – because he often used to ask the club what his net salary would be whenever he discussed a new contract with the club. The nickname returned when he came back to Ajax, albeit in a different context. This time, it was for his lack of spending. By 2015, Ajax were financially healthier than the likes of Barcelona, Manchester United and Bayern Munich when it came to operating results (profit), solvency (financial soundness) and liquid assets (cash), which is a credit to them, but their lack of reinvestment in the playing squad was a cause of frustration.

Some believed it was down to Cruyff's vision of wanting to promote players from within, but the academy was going to take time having just been re-established since the revolution. Fans wanted immediate results. They had the right to believe that if the money was there, then the club should invest adequately in the first team. Losing the *Eredivisie* title to PSV in 2015 and poor performances in Europe for nearly a decade didn't help matters either. Between 2012, the year of Overmars's return, and 2015, Ajax had sold over €86m worth of talent and only brought in about €25m. Factor in the departures of Cruyff, Jonk and Ruben Jongkind and there was vast criticism towards Overmars.

The media gave him a hard time too. In October 2015, he appeared on Kees Jansma's Sunday morning sports show, *De Tafel van Kees* (Kees's Table), and his few stutters when discussing his plans and Ajax's future drew the ire. One segment about failed transfers was a particularly awkward watch.

Overmars: 'Well, um, I, we've tried maybe ten [potential transfers].'

Jansma: 'Name them.'

Overmars: 'That striker who plays in Turkey. I've lost his name. Ehh, [Óscar] Cardozo? He played for Benfica.'

Jansma: 'Yeah, sure.'

Overmars: 'Ehh.'

Jansma: 'Definitely, that big strong striker.'

Overmars: 'Ehh … Let's see, we still have … I don't have the list.'

The newspapers didn't spare Overmars in the following weeks either: 'It was hard to believe that this man, as director of the stock exchange listed multimillion company Ajax, is responsible for the transfer policy and scouting. His lack of ready knowledge stood out,' wrote Paul Onkenhout in *De Volkskrant*. Then, a few months later after no one joined Ajax in the winter transfer window of 2016, Onkenhout spoke out again: 'And then there are those who find it strange that Ajax show no decisiveness on the player market. The excerpt from *De Tafel van Kees* was circulated again on Monday by furious Ajax supporters who have been bored to death in the Arena for years and are especially pissed about the fact that they are saddled with worthless players, while the club is €100m in the plus [on the balance sheet].'

Controversy arose over a conflict of interest issue when an interior design company, ZO!interieurprojecten, owned by Overmars's brother-in-law, was called in to refurbish De Toekomst. According to Ajax there was no unethical behaviour, but leaked emails from *De Volkskrant* tried to prove otherwise. Additionally, in 2013, construction company Braakman & Pannekoek were called in for renovations of the De Toekomst facility. Braakman & Pannekoek often assisted Overmars in his real estate company and they apparently received €103,000 for their work with Ajax, with leaked emails showing Overmars's approval.

According to the club's records, Ajax were aware of the transaction happening, but it didn't appear in their 2014/15 annual report. Any potential conflict of interest within a publicly listed company has to be justified in the Tabaksblat Code, which came into effect in 2003 to prevent misconduct by directors. The club, however, defended Overmars throughout and the case was put behind them.

The pressure was on and, while there weren't immediate results, what did catch the eye was the vision for the future. There were some key long-term signings, or signings Ajax hoped would come good for the coming years. Arkadiusz

Milik was one of the high-profile ones having joined on loan and then a €2.8m fee in 2015. His two years saw him score 47 goals and brought a €32m sale to Napoli in 2016. André Onana (€150,000), Amin Younes (€2.5m) and Lasse Schöne (free) were other sensible transfers. Frenkie de Jong's was probably the masterpiece. With the board reluctant to pay €1m for the player, Overmars discussed a paltry €1 fee with a ten per cent sell-on bonus to Willem II.

This was now Ajax and inspired by Van der Sar and Overmars. There's input from those more experienced around them, from those that didn't spend about half their lives on a football pitch, but the two former Ajax heroes are leading the charge. Are they doing things in the exact way Cruyff wanted? No – they have their own way of tackling issues and making a difference and they make their mistakes, but the essence is there. They've changed things, taken a different direction and with that comes risk.

Helping Ajax return to the top is a long process, as Overmars's experiences showed. The first task was to clean up the mess left behind, then to start building up, and while frustrations often arose over the drawn-out nature of the task, there was always a feeling that this was never going to be a quick fix. One of their big early decisions together came in the form of Peter Bosz, the head coach appointed immediately after De Boer stepped down from his role in the summer of 2016.

This was the new Ajax, very much different to the one they had become popular for, but still retaining some of the core values of old. The revolution was started by Cruyff, but now, after the initial years of learning and adapting, it was time for Overmars and Van der Sar to lead the charge.

THE MAN FROM APELDOORN

Charting the rise of Peter Bosz

APELDOORN HAS a rich history. Towards the end of the 16th century, the Dutch city started to grow in popularity for its improving paper industry and housing ancestry of the Dutch royal family. It was in 1684 that Willem III van Oranje bought house Het Loo and built Palace Het Loo, where several members of the royal family have stayed on numerous occasions. Nowadays, it's a hotspot for tranquillity. Apeldoorn's calm and space appeals to many, and sport has found its way too. From volleyball to indoor athletics to cycling and football, Apeldoorn is modern, and it's paved the way for sporting minds to rise.

Peter Bosz is Apeldoorn born and bred. In his home there lies a box of notes filled with tactical writings compiled by the former midfielder and written down over the course of his 18-year playing career. The most frequent figure in these notes is Rinus Michels, who coached Bosz at Euro 1992, when they were part of the Netherlands national team set-up.

'It is very difficult for me to throw things away, so I still have those notebooks from the Euro 92 in Sweden,' Bosz once said. 'I didn't think I was good enough for the Dutch national team. I was in the team with Ruud Gullit, Frank Rijkaard and Marco van Basten and when Rinus Michels did his match discussions he often really highlighted one aspect. For example, why the Italian defenders were so good. Immediately after such a meeting, I walked to my hotel room and wrote it all down, knowing that this would come in handy. I knew I was not good enough as a player, but maybe later as a coach [they would be useful].'

Bosz started his playing career with local side AGOVV's amateurs, before moving to the CIOS in Arnhem – a famous sports school in the Netherlands – at the age of 16, where Vitesse paid for his living costs while he trained. He made his debut for the club against Feyenoord at the age of 17 but refused to sign a professional contract with them as he insisted on a clause that would let him move on once his contract expired, to which Vitesse refused to bow. Two years later, Bosz bought out his own contract using money he gathered from friends and family, going over to RKC Waalwijk.

In between his playing career, Bosz also spent time being a salesman to make ends meet. He used to drive a company car to industrial estates and try to convince employers there that buying fuel cards for their employees would be more cost-effective. However, he wasn't very good at it, with football being his greatest strength. After Waalwijk, he went abroad, playing in France and Germany before two stints in Japan with JEF United, where he ended his career in 1999. After his foreign adventures, Bosz returned home to AGOVV for the start of his coaching career, and he was inspired by the idea of high-pressure, attacking football – something he admired after frequently watching the Ajax teams of Johan Cruyff in the 1980s and then secretly observing Louis van Gaal's Ajax sides train when they were in their best years in the 1990s, while he played for fierce rivals Feyenoord.

The amateur title at AGOVV in 2002 was a fine start and it was a place where he had the freedom to make big decisions such as on recruitment and training, but that momentum was soon gone when he joined De Graafschap, his next club, who were relegated from the *Eerste Divisie*. Soon, he would find himself at Heracles Almelo, once again in the Dutch second division, who took notice of Bosz's footballing ideas and gave him a chance. In his first season at the club (2004/05), Bosz led Heracles to promotion, and in the *Eredivisie*, they achieved a respectable 13th-place finish as the coach received plaudits for his side's playing style.

Bosz preferred keeping the ball on the ground and playing their way out of trouble rather than thumping it out of pressure. Additionally, their slick passing and organised forward movement was also noteworthy. For the players, his half-time team talks were another point that stood out. Inspired by former coach and World Cup runner-up in 1974 and 1978, Wim Jansen, who Bosz worked with at Feyenoord in the early 1990s, Bosz picked up the skills for an impactful team talk, identifying that coaches don't have to discuss things throughout the 15 minutes, but instead, giving players the space to think and recuperate in their break.

He stayed quiet for most of the 15 minutes, knowing that players wouldn't fully grasp what was said in the initial minutes of the break. As players got calmer towards the end of the break, he provided a succinct analysis of the first half and what was to be done in the second. 'Believe me: I have seen enough coaches who started talking at minute one until minute 13 in the break. You just don't know what was said in the first minutes. Bosz briefly explains his analysis of the first half and what we had to do differently after the break. That was enlightening,' his former player, Antoine van der Linden, said to *Tubantia*. Mark Looms, who worked with Bosz at Heracles, also added to that, telling me Bosz wanted the players to find solutions: 'He always asked what we thought about matches, and he helped the team using that – he wanted us to find solutions to problems as well. It was always in a tactical way. We discussed that with each other [amongst the players] at half-time and then tried to implement that in the second half.'

Bosz's spell at Heracles lasted just two fruitful years, after which he returned to Feyenoord in 2006, the club for whom he played over 150 matches as a player. This time, though, he didn't go there as a coach. Instead, he became their technical director, overseeing their policy as they looked to return to the pinnacle of Dutch football. Bosz's time at Feyenoord was tumultuous, unlike his spell there as a player. With heavy investment into the squad in his two and a half years there, the Rotterdam club purchased Roy Makaay, Giovanni van Bronckhorst and Tim de Cler, amongst others. There was a lack of stability at the club, and the team was affected too mainly because of the constant turnover in coaching staff.

In his time, three different head coaches were brought in and, after an outlay of close to €26m, the lack of success was concerning. Although Feyenoord won the KNVB Cup in 2008, they finished seventh in the league twice and sixth once, only qualifying for the UEFA Cup on one occasion and barely making a mark amongst the top sides. Erwin Koeman was the first head coach under Bosz but he was let go early and replaced on an interim basis by Leo

Beenhakker. Bert van Marwijk took over in 2007, won the cup and left a year later to be replaced by Gertjan Verbeek, who failed to make a mark.

In January 2009, some two and a half years after joining, Bosz would leave after Verbeek was let go. The spell was widely criticised, but Bosz thought of it as a crucial learning curve: 'When I was technical director at Feyenoord, I went abroad a lot; a lot in Brazil, a lot at the top clubs in England. I spoke with Arsène Wenger from Arsenal, those kinds of great trainers. You rarely get that chance as a coach because you're just really busy,' he later said to NOS about his spell at Feyenoord. To get back on track, he made a return to Heracles not long after, and Bosz's return there was far better.

Now an established *Eredivisie* club, Bosz would elevate Heracles with exciting, attacking football, rather than focusing on stern defending to get results, like he did in his first stint in Almelo. The mentality of winning 3-2 rather than 1-0 was apparent over the next few years as Heracles were always keen on moving forward and playing with intensity. Over three seasons, they finished eighth once and 12th twice, even reaching the KNVB Cup Final in 2012, where they lost to PSV Eindhoven – a strong return for a club that didn't have a vast history in the *Eredivisie*.

At Heracles, Bosz also met and worked with Peter Blangé, the former Dutch volleyball player who starred for them at four Olympic Games. Blangé introduced him to data tools like SportVU, a tracking system that allowed coaches to monitor their players' physical performance, improve their insight, prevent injuries and create better training methods. First used in the NBA in 2010 by franchises such as the Dallas Mavericks (who went on to win the championship that season), Houston Rockets, Oklahoma City Thunder and the San Antonio Spurs, it soon made its way to football.

According to Bosz, it helped him learn how to better his players' positioning and sustain compactness when defending. This was a tool that would aid Bosz throughout his coaching career. Of course, Bosz would still believe much of coaching was still down to what he saw with his own eyes, and he employed a big team of data and video analysts, but according to him it was still 95 per cent based on what he saw, and 5 per cent based on what he was supplemented with through data.

Looms remembers his time working under Bosz at Heracles fondly: 'He was a very tactical coach. When he speaks about football, everybody is inspired, and we listened to him with such respect. When he speaks, you feel the way he feels about football. He always believes in attacking football. We always need to have the ball and we should think about our strengths. At Heracles, we are a smaller club compared to others and when we played against clubs like Ajax, Feyenoord or PSV we always believed that we were better. When we go on the pitch or warm up, we wanted to believe we could win the game. We were a little club, but when we had meetings with the team, he always empowered us. Training was always intense. He always wanted high intensity. Whenever we came into the club, from the first moment, you must be at the highest intensity on the pitch and in the dressing room we always had to be focused.'

Much of Bosz's career thus far was filled with returns, and he would make another at Vitesse, coming back to the club in 2013 – 29 years after he left, this time as head coach. In Arnhem, he carried the club forward and many in the

Ajax celebrate winning the 1995 Champions League title. Matters would drastically change for the club soon after that success.

Ajax were modernising and moving to the Amsterdam Arena in 1996 was central to that.

Johan Cruyff's revolution at Ajax involved plenty of infighting, back-stabbing, appointments and sackings. Here he is at court.

Part of Camp Cruyff in this revolution were two famous Ajax figures, Dennis Bergkamp and Wim Jonk.

Amidst all the changes, Ajax ended their seven-year title drought in 2011, beating FC Twente on the final day of the season to win the Eredivisie.

Post-revolution, Marc Overmars was heavily involved with Ajax, helping his club to four successive league title wins.

Edwin van der Sar was involved in marketing before being bumped up to CEO.

Under Peter Bosz, Ajax put together an impressive run to the Europa League Final with a young team.

Erik ten Hag joined in 2017 and with his own special style, he spearheaded a magical Ajax team.

The signings of Dušan Tadić and Daley Blind in the summer of 2018 signalled the start of a new transfer policy for Ajax.

The signings were complemented by talented academy graduates, such as future captain Matthijs de Ligt and Donny van de Beek.

In the 2018/19 season, Ajax's wonderful Champions League run to the semi-finals captured the hearts of many.

David Neres and Antony were two examples of Ajax's hunt for gifted South American players.

In 2012, Ajax also started their women's team, becoming one of the most popular sides in the Dutch Vrouwen Eredivisie.

Johan Cruyff's death in 2016 saddened many, and his legacy is still remembered throughout Amsterdam.

Ajax won the league title in 2019 after a five-year drought and have consistently been the Netherlands' best club since.

country believed Bosz's side played the best football in the *Eredivisie*. Within five months of joining, Vitesse were top of the league for the first time since 2006; however, a slump in the second half of the campaign resigned them to a sixth-place finish. The squad was young too and helped heavily by owner Alexandr Chigirinsky's good relationship with Roman Abramovich, the owner of Chelsea, and the London side often used that link to loan young footballers there.

From Lucas Piazón to Bertrand Traoré, many found their feet at Vitesse under the instinctive Bosz as Vitesse continued to improve. His teams were talented and flexible, often deploying a 4-3-3, 4-2-4 or a 4-4-2, being able to transition during games and adapt for certain situations. Bosz was helped by assistant Albert Capellas – the former Barcelona assistant who worked with Pep Guardiola during the treble-winning 2008/09 season – crediting the Spaniard for teaching him about the intricacies of positional play and how he never starts training sessions with a warm-up, instead playing a small game with emphasis on positioning. The Dutchman believes the risk of injury without a warm-up is far less than many anticipate, and a game is just as beneficial.

Indeed, Guardiola, a disciple of Cruyff, was also a big influence on Bosz and the Dutchman later spoke about the impact Capellas and Guardiola had on his career. Talking to *Trouw*: 'I don't have much time to read, but *Herr Pep* [or *Pep Confidential*, by Martí Perarnau], is the best book I have ever read. It's an inspiring book. When Barcelona played, we would watch Barcelona with all the coaches on TV as often as possible … I have seen Albert Capellas at Vitesse. He was one of the assistants and had worked with Guardiola at Barcelona for many years. I learned so much from that man.'

Bosz's second season was better, as Vitesse stayed close to the top three throughout, and ended up qualifying for the Europa League, earning him a nomination for the Rinus Michels Award, given to the best coach in the Netherlands. That ended up going to Phillip Cocu of league-winning PSV Eindhoven, but it was a worthy reward for a job very well done. That would be Bosz's last full season at Vitesse as, in January 2016, he would make a rather unconventional move to Israel to take over at Maccabi Tel Aviv. There, Jordi Cruyff was making a mark having been their sporting director since 2013 and he was looking for a Cruyff-like vision to take the club forward. Bosz was the ideal man for that, and it brought him closer to Johan, his greatest influence.

The belief was that Cruyff wanted Maccabi to be Israel's version of Ajax – a club constantly ahead of the competition, able to dominate their domestic league and producing top-quality young footballers while maintaining a defined, attractive style of football. Bosz was seen as the right candidate to lead the team forward, and with the club having recently played Champions League football, the coach saw this as a good opportunity too. After Cruyff's arrival in 2012, Maccabi won the domestic title three times on the bounce and Bosz, taking over mid-season, was expected to lay the foundations for another era of success, with Cruyff admitting early on that Bosz was a long-term target for the club.

At Maccabi, Johan Cruyff was a frequent visitor, invited by his son and owner Mitch Goldhar, who used to say he would share his vision on the game and advise the club. Shortly before his death on 24 March 2016, Bosz spent a week learning and talking to the Barcelona and Ajax legend.

On the day of Cruyff's death, Bosz spoke about meeting Cruyff to *Voetbal International*: 'Johan was and still is the greatest player the Netherlands has had. He had his own idea about how football should be played. In my active career I have learned a lot from Johan. And later as a coach it was a privilege to meet him and to spend a week with him recently. We talked about football every day.' Bosz later admitted that spending a week with Johan gave him ten years' worth of footballing education.

Bosz's spell in Israel was short-lived. Maccabi finished runners-up in the league, three points behind champions Hapoel Be'er Sheva, while they also lost the Israeli State Cup Final to Maccabi Haifa. However, that didn't affect Bosz's reputation, given that he had only joined mid-season.

He was gone soon after, given that there was a clause in his contract that allowed him to move to Ajax whenever they came calling, and in the summer after joining, he was on his way back home, taking on the biggest job in his career at the biggest club in the Netherlands. Whether Jordi himself influenced the move is unknown, but there certainly was Johan's influence in Bosz that made Ajax feel he was a worthy candidate.

His Feyenoord links made it difficult for fans to accept his arrival, with many against the idea of it, but his style of football was something that appealed to the club. Speaking at a KNVB coaching conference in 2017, *Voor het voetbal* (For football), he explained some key fundamentals to his management. Bosz's presentation was about how to create a winning team, and he believed there was no single way to success for coaches and a lot depended on variables:

- The culture of the club that you are presently working at

- The coaches you work with

- The players you have at your disposal

Additionally, he also explained the key principles to his playing style:

- High pressure on the opponents: 'Players have to understand that, so I need intelligent football players. I am not afraid that we will be one on one at the back by putting pressure on. I only get scared when we can't put pressure on the ball anymore.'

- Compact play: 'You can only put high pressure if you are compact. Every coach will recognise the importance of that, but the big question is: how do you do that? How do you make such a general statement concrete? It comes down to making the field small when the ball is played over you, and you have to have the courage. The latter is something I, as a trainer, work on a lot.'

- Five-second rule: 'Being compact also means that you switch immediately from the moment you lose the ball. I call it the five-second rule. If the opponent conquers the ball, it takes them about five seconds to "get big again" and play the ball around again. Within that time, we want to conquer the ball again. This means that the players closest to the ball must pressure them immediately. The other players should make the field small, so they shouldn't be running backwards. The basic principle of this type of defence is that the opponent does not matter. After all, if you give a mediocre footballer time, he will automatically become a good player.

Conversely, if you put pressure on a good footballer, his qualities will rarely show.'

He was ready to bring all that to Amsterdam. Above all on the pitch, football was for the fans, and Bosz understood that. Speaking to *Deutsche Welle*, Bosz wanted the fans to enjoy what they were watching: 'That's connected with emotions. I like to watch teams where something happens. Playing wide, playing backward, only playing long passes, that doesn't belong to the football that I love. I want to cheer when I watch football. It should be fun to watch. That also is why I try to let my team play in a way that the fans like.' This was the new Ajax with Marc Overmars and Edwin van der Sar leading the boardroom, and they chose Bosz as the man to take them forward on the pitch.

FROM AMSTERDAM TO STOCKHOLM

The 2016/17 season, a new start for Ajax

ROSTOV-ON-DON, 24 August 2016. Ajax travel to Russia for the second leg of their Champions League play-off match against Rostov, having drawn 1-1 in Amsterdam. They wish to be in the Champions League competition proper, having missed out in the previous season, but the spirits around the club aren't high. The end of the Frank de Boer era still stings, and there is anger directed at Marc Overmars for his refusal to spend money in the transfer market. Matters don't get any better at full time. Sardar Azmoun scores for the home side in the first half, and then in the second a quick flurry of goals from Aleksandr Yerokhin, Christian Noboa and Dmitry Poloz give Rostov an unassailable 4-0 lead. Even Davy Klaasen's late consolation penalty doesn't draw any positives: Ajax fail to make it to the group stages of the Champions League again.

Joël Veltman, who had been with Ajax since 2001 and with the senior team since 2012, knows the culture at the club. He was previously part of league-winning teams, and he knew that the fans didn't enjoy the ending to that spell.

He tells me that after the loss to Rostov, the pressure on the players and around the club only increased: 'At Ajax, there's always a bit of negativity because of the expectations. You have to win matches, you have to play in the Champions League and you have to win the league title every year. If you didn't do it in the year before, there's more pressure to do it in the year after. In the Netherlands, not many people knew Rostov. We heard the name and knew a few of the players but that was it and they beat us, so there was even more pressure after that game.'

The season was new, but Bosz was already feeling the heat. The ex-Feyenoord man had plenty to appease to and the Champions League exit only made his job tougher. He did get the benefit of the doubt, though. The investment wasn't adequate, and there was a general belief that the talents coming through the academy needed more time to acclimatise to senior football. Bosz's first transfer window in charge was difficult: interest was there in Twente's Hakim Ziyech, but the Enschede club's €11m asking price put Ajax off. There was also the sale of Polish forward Arkadiusz Milik, Ajax's main source of goals, who went to Napoli for €32m despite the club saying he would stay in Amsterdam. A player that did come in was Bertrand Traoré, who joined on loan from Chelsea – another source of annoyance amongst fans given that he was a temporary signing – and also Davinson Sánchez, the Copa Libertadores-winning defender from Atlético Nacional.

The Champions League exit combined with a dire league start, which included a home draw against Roda JC and away defeat at Willem II, changed things. Goalkeeper Jasper Cillessen was on the move, going to Barcelona, and on the arrivals front, Ziyech's price tag was no longer considered hefty, joining late in the window. It was a panic buy and Overmars, at the end of the season, admitted his error – the club acted slowly and wanted to streamline the process of signing players in the future.

As expected, Bosz wanted to make use of the players coming through the academy and Jong Ajax (the second team, playing in the second division) as well and the complicated transfer window accelerated that process: Kasper Dolberg already had a good reputation at the club, André Onana, the former La Masia goalkeeper, was expected to be the replacement for Cillessen, while the likes of Matthijs de Ligt, Donny van de Beek, Frenkie de Jong, Justin Kluivert and Abdelhak Nouri were eyeing more chances in the first team. A lot of credit for this had to go to Marcel Keizer, the coach of Jong Ajax who nurtured these talents.

On the pitch, things started to improve after the Champions League exit. The home defeat against Willem II in the league was the last they would suffer for a while and on all fronts Peter Bosz's side would show maturity beyond their years. A KNVB Cup win against Willem II in late September was the turning point. This was when De Ligt, De Jong and Nouri made their debuts with the first team, and it set the blueprint for the rest of the season. Towards the end of De Boer's tenure, Ajax had become timider, lacking any real intensity and having possession for the sake of it, but it was from here that matters changed: more risk, playing higher up the pitch, closing the opposition down and making the best of Bosz's emphasised five-second rule.

Although they didn't want to be in the competition, the Europa League was a useful tournament for this group of players and, placed in Group G alongside Panathinaikos,

Standard Liège and Celta Vigo, the Amsterdam side were comfortable: six matches, four wins and two draws. Veltman: 'The group stage was where we grew as a team. We were winning a lot. I remember the home games well because we were able to score a lot of goals, but it was a bit more complicated in the away games. We had a good feeling amongst the team after the group stage and had a manager like Bosz who planned everything well for us. He often used to tell us to pay attention to his plans and follow him. We were young, so we followed his advice.'

There were some unique experiences for the team too. In the game against Standard Liège at the Amsterdam Arena, Ajax won 1-0, but it was the scenes in the stands that caught the eye: the away fans had flares thrown on to the lower sections of the stadium where children and families were seated, causing disruptions. In the return fixture, the Ajax fans hit back with flares of their own, launching them on to the pitch within five minutes of kick-off, forcing the game to be halted temporarily. Having already won the group by the time this December game was played, this was a younger team, with many getting their first taste of European football.

The clashes against Celta Vigo brought the almost inevitable breakthrough of Dolberg. The Dane, who had long been admired by Overmars having been signed after just one trial, used the group phase as a chance to show off his talents. In Vigo, a 2-2 draw, Dolberg set up Ziyech for a goal and in the return fixture, a 3-2 win, he got on the scoresheet himself. It was also in these fixtures that Bosz was able to discover his strongest side, which became a more frequent line-up after the winter break when the season really got into gear. This was the midfield of Klaassen,

Lasse Schöne and Ziyech and the front three of Traoré, Dolberg and Amin Younes.

'He was very good in what he was planning with us,' Veltman says about Bosz. 'He's one of my favourite coaches and that was because he had a plan and he stuck with it throughout the season. There were no exemptions. He had a really clear idea of how to press opponents, how to work with the ball, and we really liked his work. I had never been so fit until I played under him, and I really enjoyed working with him.' It was the attention to detail that made Bosz such an immediate hit in Amsterdam. By December, Ajax had comfortably won their Europa League group, were still in the title race and had a chance in the cup too. After a complex start, there was some optimism amongst fans that great things could be achieved.

However, it was in December where they suffered the first real slump under Bosz and the first blow they would suffer in their title bid. A loss to Twente and a draw against PSV just before Christmas gave Feyenoord an advantage, while they also suffered a cup defeat against Cambuur. In the new year, the team really started to shape up. Taking inspiration from the Celta Vigo clashes, Ajax became an attacking force domestically and in Europe. At the back, Onana was growing in confidence, Sánchez, only 20, was easing into European football while De Ligt was backed for great things. The midfield of Klaasen, Schöne and Ziyech was particularly impressive. The three had unique attributes that made them function so well together: Klaasen, the captain, brought the balance and popped up with several important goals that season, Ziyech was the creative force while Schöne was improving as the playmaker, always looking to move the ball forward.

Ajax were scoring freely and were solid at the back – like how they should be – and in the Europa League they faced Poland's Legia Warsaw in the round of 32. After a stern 0-0 draw away, Nick Viergever, who was becoming more and more important to Bosz, scored the sole goal to send Ajax through. The second leg saw Ajax being more sloppy and far too predictable in attack. Viergever's goal in the 49th minute allowed the home side to take more control, establishing dominance in the midfield and hardly giving Legia a chance. They knew one away goal for the Warsaw side would send them out, but Ajax never gave them that chance. Bosz's side were through to the round of 16 to face Copenhagen, and the events of that spring would never have been imagined at the start of the season.

Back in the Netherlands, there was another small slump in March and April, which effectively made a difference in the title race. In this close battle with Feyenoord, every dropped point would alter proceedings, and those points were dropped in Ajax's bid to have a fine European run. On 5 March 2017, just four days before Ajax's first-leg clash against Copenhagen, Groningen held the Amsterdammers to a 1-1 draw. In Denmark, Ajax lost 2-1. Dolberg scored the away goal in his home nation, and towards the end had a goal ruled out.

In the second leg, the Amsterdam Arena once again provided a boost. Traoré levelled scores midway through the first half, while towards the end of the half, Dolberg was on target again, this time from the penalty spot, to give Ajax the lead. De Ligt and Sánchez were unscathed at the back and for the first time since 2003 – 14 years prior – Ajax were in the last eight of a European competition. Out of all the talent coming through, Veltman rated Dolberg the highest: 'Kasper Dolberg: he's amazing,' the Dutch defender says. 'It was his first year in the team and he was reaching a new level. He used to score in most games, he was technical, he had speed, a lot of strength and had a good shot. I was disappointed when he left eventually, but at the time, Dolberg was my favourite.'

In the last eight, the competition would really step up: Schalke were drawn. The season was already becoming a historic one. In previous years, fans had already got used to not having European football at this stage of the campaign; the football was dire and season-ticket renewal numbers were going down, but Bosz had brought Ajax back to the level they were known to be on. Indeed, the Europa League didn't have the same prestige as the Champions League, but in this uneven footballing landscape where the Champions League was the playground of the billionaires, this Europa League run brought plenty of pride back to the club and city.

Ajax were hoping for a league and European double, and going into the first leg against Schalke, they were in solid form: three wins on the bounce, 11 goals scored and three conceded. Against Schalke, Bosz sent out a team with an average age of exactly 22. A few players who ideally would've been there missed out through injuries or suspension, but in this crucial fixture, Bosz stuck to his guns:

Ajax starting 11 vs Schalke, Europa League quarter-final first leg (age in brackets): *Onana (21), Veltman (25), Viergever (27), Sánchez (20), Sinkgraven (21), Van de Beek (19), Ziyech (24), Klaasen (24), Kluivert (17), Traoré (21), Younes (23)*

That team's oldest player was 27 (Viergever), there were nine players aged 21 or under and four teenagers featured, with two starting (Van de Beek and Kluivert) and two coming on as substitutes (De Ligt and De Jong). Despite their youthfulness, Ajax's attacking prowess proved to be too much to handle for Schalke. Klaasen scored twice, the first from the penalty spot, and put Ajax into a healthy position ahead of the second leg in Gelsenkirchen.

If they thought the return fixture would be smooth sailing, they were wrong. After a goalless first half, Ajax were hopeful, but two goals in three minutes early in the second cancelled out Ajax's lead, and the tie would go to extra time. Daniel Caliguiri added a third for the German club and it felt the inevitable was happening: the dream was done. But Viergever, who had shown up in important moments in this season, scored the most bizarre goal, deflecting an intended Schalke clearance off his shin to give Ajax the away goal and a path to the last four. Towards the end, Younes sealed the victory. Ajax lost the game but won 4-3 on aggregate.

Veltman, who was sent off in the second leg, thought it was a marvel Ajax went through: 'We made it to extra time against Schalke and they took the lead at one point. They were going to the next round and then we put in a cross into the box and Nick Viergeiver – I don't know how he managed to do it – the ball went into the net, and everyone went crazy. We were a bit lucky and then Amin Younes ended the game. It was a miracle we went through the game.'

Just three days after the tense 120 minutes against Schalke, a spirited Ajax fell to PSV in the league, putting them in the back seat in the hunt for the league title with just two games to go. All eyes were now on the Europa League and only Lyon stood between them and a first European final in 21 years. Once again, cautious optimism took over

Amsterdam. They were helped by the fact that Lyon's star forward, Alexandre Lacazette, was to miss the first leg at home. The team sent out for that fixture was younger than the one that played against Schalke. Schöne was the oldest at 30, De Ligt, at 17, was the youngest, and the average age of the starting 11 dropped to 21.8:

> Ajax starting 11 vs Lyon, Europa League semi-final first leg: *Onana (21), Tete (21), Sánchez (20), De Ligt (17), Riedewald (20), Ziyech (24), Klaasen (24), Schöne (30), Traoré (21), Younes (23), Dolberg (19)*

Wednesday, 3 May 2017, the night Ajax felt like they were in their place. The match finished 4-1; there was a party in the city at half-time when they were up 2-0 at half-time. Traoré scored twice, once in either half; Dolberg and Younes scored the other two goals, Ziyech assisted three. They were quick, playing at a different pace to their French opposition, playing as though they had been at this level for years, but that wasn't the case. Bosz had instilled a different mentality and confidence into the team – they played without fear, like they had nothing to lose.

Dick Sintnie, writing in *Het Parool* after the match, believed this was an Ajax that the late Johan Cruyff would've been proud of: 'Even fifteen minutes after the final whistle, the stadium was packed to thank the Ajax footballers for an unforgettable evening during their lap of honour. They even received a standing ovation from the Lyon supporters. But the rest of football-loving Europe will also have seen Ajax play with a happy feeling.'

And while that fearless mentality benefitted them, in the away tie in France it almost cost them. This time, Ajax lost 3-1, despite scoring early through Dolberg. Viergever's sending off made things more difficult, but they held on. Ajax, through the trials and tribulations, were through. Bosz had led Ajax to a tenth European final in their history, and this was amongst the most unlikely. After Keith Spurgeon, Rinus Michels, Ştefan Kovács, Cruyff, Barry Hulshoff and Louis van Gaal, Bosz became the sixth coach to lead Ajax to a major continental final.

From the knockout rounds onwards, there was a trend emerging: Ajax were struggling in away games. They hadn't won an away knockout match, drawing one and losing three, once requiring extra time. In the round of 32, they drew 0-0 against Legia Warsaw. Then in Copenhagen, they lost 2-1. Schalke and Lyon beat them 3-2 and 3-1, respectively. Was this young side more fazed by away games? Veltman: 'I think that was the case. Our home games were crazy with the fans, and they were giving us the support but on the other side, in the away games, because we were young, we had a bit of trouble because the opposition used to score an early goal or come at us with lots of pressure. They had the same power as we did when they were with their fans and we were young so maybe we didn't handle it in the right way, so that was a disadvantage, and you could often see that in the results.'

Ajax gave the total football of old a modern touch: the circulation of the ball was quick and precise, defenders knew how to move the ball forward, opponents were chased down to the end. Most importantly, this was engaging to the fans. It wasn't too long ago that they were tired of the dull football and, while this season wasn't guaranteed to bring trophies, it was a successful season as they were able to regain their identity of old and do it by promoting from within. Going into the final day of the *Eredivisie* season, Ajax were a point behind Feyenoord, who were chasing a first national championship in 18 years. The Amsterdam side had scored the second-most goals in the league, after Feyenoord, and conceded the joint fewest, along with PSV Eindhoven. The dream was there, but they fell just short: Feyenoord won their match against Heracles, and Ajax did their best, beating Willem II and securing an 81-point domestic campaign, which was more than what any of De Boer's title-winning sides ever got to.

All their hopes were now pinned on the Europa League. Ajax had been across Europe in this run. Spain, Greece and Belgium in the group stage; Poland, Denmark, France and Germany in the knockout rounds. An English club, Manchester United, were the final hurdle, and there were big differences between the two.

The summer before the season started, in addition to appointing José Mourinho as head coach, Manchester United had spent €185m on transfers, including the world-record €105m purchase of Paul Pogba from Juventus. Ajax had spent nearly that amount in the previous decade. There were differences in finances, quality of talent, the experience of their respective squads and résumés of their respective head coaches: Mourinho was a three-time European title winner and had never lost a European final; Bosz had never been in a cup final in his managerial career. There was a clear favourite, even though the Red Devils' domestic season was less than convincing.

In the Friends Arena in Stockholm, like in previous rounds, there was another young team sent out in the hope of bringing back Ajax's first continental honour since Van Gaal's Ajax beat Milan in the Champions League Final of 1995, which was coincidentally played on the same date as the 2017 final: 24 May. Bosz named the youngest team to ever take the field in a European final with an average age of 22.18. This included De Ligt, the youngest-ever player to start a European final, and just two players who were 25 or over.

> Ajax starting 11 vs Manchester United, Europa League Final: *Onana (21), Veltman (25), Sánchez (20), De Ligt (17), Riedewald (20), Klaasen (24), Schöne (30), Ziyech (24), Traoré (21), Younes (23), Dolberg (19)*

In the final, experience prevailed. Pogba scored early on – his heavily deflected shot flummoxed Onana to give United the lead. Early in the second-half, Henrikh Mkhitaryan, another summer signing, doubled United's lead. The match was difficult: Mourinho asked the tall and troublesome Marouane Fellaini to disrupt Ajax's midfield, and the Belgian obliged. Matteo Darmian, who had a stop-start career at Old Trafford, had the game of his life at full-back. Daley Blind, the ex-*Ajacied*, did a fine job at centre-half too, unruffled for the most part.

Van der Sar, who played for both clubs, had a soft spot for both, but said it would only be a dream if Ajax won. That wasn't to be the case, but there was still pride and emotion. Ajax had now laid the foundations for the future. Manchester United and Mourinho did it in their way, nullifying Ajax, and in 13 previous finals for Mourinho, he'd only lost twice. He knew a way to win. 'If you want to press the ball all the time, you don't play short. If you are dominant in the air, you go long,' the Portuguese said after the match to BT Sport. 'There are lots of poets in football but poets, they don't win many titles.'

Veltman recognised that the mountain was too high as well. Fellaini was a problem to deal with, and United's know-how was a big game changer. 'It was the same preparation for Manchester United as it was in previous matches against Lyon and Schalke,' he says. 'We felt Manchester United were a different level compared to Lyon or Schalke and we didn't deserve much out of that game. The first goal for them had a bit of luck – Paul Pogba's shot kept changing directions in the last moments. But, you know, with José Mourinho, if you go down 1-0, they will kill the game and we couldn't do anything. They had Marouane Fellaini in front, which was a big difference. I was talking to Daley Blind after the game and he was telling me, "If I play it short, Mourinho would shout at me, asking me to play it long to Fellaini," and that sort of thing. He [Blind] was surprised by that, but that was their idea of playing – just pass it long to Fellaini: he was so strong in the air and was able to carry the play forward from there. They killed the game after they went 1-0 up early.'

Would it have been different if this Ajax side had have been together for longer or had more experience? Veltman: 'Maybe. In the end, we accepted that we lost because Manchester United, with all their experience, were a challenge. Even if we had three or four more years together, it's also about quality and I think Manchester United are a bigger name and have more money to buy quality players. You never know. It's one game and it's a final, so we may have been better, but we'll never know. After the game, everyone was disappointed, but the feeling of pride came days after.'

Veltman was a part of the De Boer era. He had been around for a while, enjoyed success and seen fine, young players come through. But the belief for fans was that for the first time in a long time, this felt like the Ajax of old, like how they should be. Does Veltman think the same? 'Yes and no. At the time, we were champions quite often. In the Champions League, we didn't do too well, playing against tough teams in the group stages, but not getting beyond the group stage or going far in the Europa League. Yes, we were doing great domestically, but not so well in Europe, and this was the year we were playing well in Europe but not as well domestically, so it's difficult to say. But it was where we wanted to be with Ajax – even at the European stage, we wanted to be at the highest level.'

He continues, saying reaching the final was the best part about that season: 'Feyenoord won the championship that year after 18 years and we were really close. They played well and had a lot of luck too, but you have one of those years where other teams aren't at the same level of quality. Everything fell into place for them and, because of the games we played in the Europa League when we made it to the final, we had a lot of matches to play, so we were often focusing on the quarter-finals, semi-finals or final as well as the league. That [losing the league] was disappointing but making it to the final was the best thing.'

Hope and pride were the common themes that season, but after a great campaign, there was always an inkling that the vultures from abroad would circle around their top players. Klaasen was already expected to leave, and he found his way to Everton that summer. Sánchez earned a €42m move to Tottenham, making him the most expensive Ajax departure ever after just one incredible season at the club. Traoré would return to Chelsea after his season-long loan spell, but the most irksome departure was that of coach

Bosz, who would move to Borussia Dortmund. At the same time of his departure, stories were out about his rifts with the management: his assistants Hennie Spijkerman and Dennis Bergkamp weren't on the best of terms with him because Bosz mainly discussed matters with Henrie Krüzen, who he had been working with for years at previous clubs.

In later interviews, Bosz revealed some of the conversations he had with Bergkamp and pointed out that the ex-Arsenal player often brought up his playing career, saying Bosz never played at a top club other than Feyenoord. The belief was that Overmars wanted Bosz to stay, and Bergkamp didn't, while Van der Sar had no preference but ultimately picked Bergkamp's side, paving the way for Bosz's move to Germany. Jong Ajax head coach Keizer was seen as the ideal replacement – he had worked with much of the squad and the youngsters coming through previously, but yet another power struggle after such a positive campaign was infuriating. Veltman says the players wanted Bosz to stick around for longer: 'I heard about the disputes between him and the rest of the management. As players, we wanted him to stay. He used to have discussions over his assistants. Bosz wanted different people to work with him, but Ajax said no. It had nothing to do with the players.'

The season started off with disappointment in the Champions League, but a euphoric spring made Ajax believe again. Although it ended trophy-less, there was a feeling of glory, that great things could be achieved again. Bosz's departure caused anger and confusion, but his sole season would be remembered for a while. The man from Apeldoorn, the ex-Feyenoorder, had done Ajax and Amsterdam proud, but it was now time for someone else.

DE TUKKER

This is Erik ten Hag

LONG BEFORE he joined Ajax at the end of 2017, Erik ten Hag was considered as the crown prince of modern Dutch coaching – a man who connected classic styles with that of a progressive 'laptop coach', someone who mixed data and statistics with what he saw on the pitch. His best attribute was understanding people, getting into the minds of footballers and seeing things the way they see it. He once said to *Voetbal International*: 'You need to know about the man behind the player. And I tell you what, I can read this from the way a player moves, the way he responds when losing the ball, when he concedes or gets fouled. I can make a picture – a broad stroke picture – of the man. And I can use this in my management. I choose a different approach per player. But that's only the start. You also need to look at the dynamics in the group. How they relate to one another. And I can see before the game what kind of match we're getting.'

Headstrong and still slightly stubborn, Ten Hag's habits can be linked back to his upbringing in Haaksbergen, in the Twente region, close to the German border. *De Tukker*, as people from that area are known, was born into a family of entrepreneurs. His father, Hennie, started as a housing agent in 1967 and became a magnate, having nine branches around the country and over a hundred employees. But success wasn't to be given to him and his two brothers; it had to be earned, and those values were ingrained from a young age. Experience to work in the field of business was necessary for his brothers, while for Erik, there was a goal-oriented path into sport. While his family didn't necessarily want to see him work in football, instead preferring a full education, they supported him when the choice was made. FC Twente was his first love.

Ten Hag's playing career was solid, if not spectacular. A fine centre-half, he had three separate spells at Twente with time spent at De Graafschap, Waalwijk and Utrecht in between and the KNVB Cup win in 2001 with the Enschede club – when Ten Hag was captain of the team – was his only major honour. The cup win was special for Twente, coming just a year after the Enschede fireworks disaster at the S.E. Fireworks depot which killed 23 people. What Ten Hag may have lacked as a player, he made up for with his intelligence and awareness, proving to be a vital part of any team he played for. He retired in 2002 at the relatively young age of 32, having made over 200 appearances for his boyhood club. Soon, he would move into coaching and as a successful man-manager with a strong emotional awareness he had qualities from an early age to have a good career.

Despite retiring from his playing career, he didn't leave Twente, working there in a coaching capacity with the club's youngsters before being bumped up to the role of Fred Rutten's assistant with the first team. He was intrigued by the mindsets of professional athletes, wishing to learn more and improve in his craft. As a youth coach, discipline and integrity were top priorities, while team building and working for each other were his main objectives. He maintained values of old – those he was raised with himself: shoes had to be black, training vests had to be folded, not thrown around. These habits were non-negotiable. Amongst his personal library, books on sports psychology such as *De Winnaar is Gezien* (The Winner is Seen) by famous Dutch sports psychologist Peter Blitz and *Effect* by Norwegian skater Johann Olav Koss are favourites. Ten Hag developed a close bond with Rutten, who would depart for Schalke in 2008, and when Steve McClaren joined as his replacement, the Englishman was quickly impressed by his new assistant's work.

Upon joining, McClaren is immediately given six sheets of notes and suggestions on the team he took over, and a day later, more come in to help him acclimatise to the task in hand. That season, they get into a title fight with AZ Alkmaar, led by Louis van Gaal, but by 11 points fall short, finishing in second. They do, however, qualify for the Champions League – a decent return for the club. That was the sole season the pair worked together and after over 20 years of supporting Twente, playing for them, working for them and assisting the first team, Ten Hag left on a sour note, joining PSV Eindhoven, where he would reunite with Rutten as his assistant. The case would go to court, as Twente hoped to be compensated for the signing of Ten Hag, but the arbitration committee ruled otherwise.

His role at PSV was similar, working with the first team and also keeping an eye on the club's emerging youngsters. He played an important role in the development of an emerging Memphis Depay, then with the youth teams at PSV, who, according to Ten Hag, needed the freedom to work his magic. So good was his work with PSV that he would soon be given a head coach role in 2012 – ten years after retiring – and that came with Go Ahead Eagles, who were boosted by the investment from Marc Overmars and looking to make the jump up after several years in the *Eerste Divisie*. Upon joining, he made changes to the club's facilities – little details that had a big impact on his work – and his attention to detail caught the eye of many around the Netherlands.

At the first training session with the Deventer club, the players got an idea of what to expect. Ten Hag was fuming after the players decided to pile their training bibs in one big bunch. He wanted three separate groups: one of yellow bibs, the other of blue and the third of orange. He also asked for extra windows to be built in his office at the training facility to improve the transparency between him and the squad and had dugouts moved slightly closer to the pitch in the stadium. Additionally, he wanted an unused storage room to be turned into a gym, something which became popular amongst fans. All of these demands and changes earned him a nickname: *De Kleine Generaal* – The Little General. 'The Go Ahead Eagles organisation was disturbed by it for the first three months [Ten Hag's demands] … But when it started to work and a top sporting climate emerged, everyone became enthusiastic,' said Edwin Mulder, the former chairman.

The football wasn't revolutionary, but it was effective. His 4-3-3 saw the Eagles pose a threat on the counter and his detailed work on the training ground, which included intensive personal sessions with players, was what made him such a revered coach. He also used the transfer market well, getting in plenty of quality on a low price to help the team, as evident by the loan signing of a young Quincy Promes from Twente, who Ten Hag previously worked with. The front line of Promes, Xander Houtkoop and Marnix Kolder was rapid, and they contributed to the club's promotion push. He also used data to maintain his players' high fitness levels, going over to a scientist in Germany to have his team's fitness analysed and help prevent injuries. Henk ten Cate, who was coaching Sparta Rotterdam in the second division at the time, even praised the Eagles' fitness, citing it as a key reason behind their success.

It was often noted that Ten Hag himself always kept his feet on the ground, focusing on the next task and leaving little time to celebrate. Good wasn't good enough and he believed satisfaction led to laziness, not just for him and his team, but around the club. The team bus had to be precise when arriving to grounds; tactical preparations before matches were long and detailed. Even though Ten Hag wasn't at Go Ahead Eagles for a long time, there was hardly a more impactful manager – he transformed the way of doing things and the rewards of that were on the pitch. Seventeen years after they last played in the *Eredivisie*, in May 2013, Go Ahead Eagles confirmed their promotion via the play-offs, beating FC Volendam, and Ten Hag announced himself as one of the brightest managers in the Netherlands.

Sadly for the club, he didn't stay for their *Eredivisie* season as an attractive proposition from Germany came around. Bayern Munich, who were entering a new era following the arrival of Pep Guardiola, were looking for a manager for their second team in the fourth division of German football, the *Regionalliga*. Ten Hag accepted, feeling it was useful to get time in Germany and learn from Guardiola, one of his coaching idols.

Ten Hag was approached having been of interest to the club's technical director, Matthias Sammer, who frequently visited Dutch clubs and their youth facilities when he worked with the *Deutscher Fußball-Bund*, the German FA. Michael Tarnat, the director of Bayern's youth teams, also kept an eye on Ten Hag's progress over the years. At the time he was recognised by Sammer and Tarnat, ten Hag was still at FC Twente, but his fine work entered Sammer's good books, and got him a job at Germany's most successful club years later having previously been invited to speak at conferences in Germany about his coaching style.

Guardiola is known for working with new and emerging coaches, and Ten Hag was up for the challenge too. Bayern wanted a more streamlined youth department, and Ten Hag's work was to be valued. His predecessor, Mehmet Scholl, left his role a year earlier than expected and he was frequently criticised for treating his job as a part-time one, often juggling his coaching duties with commentary of German league matches on national broadcaster ARD when he had the chance. Names such as Peter Herrmann, Heiko Herrlich and Stefan Effenberg were suggested for the role as Scholl's replacement, but Sammer was adamant on bringing in Ten Hag.

One of the objectives was to take the second team as high up the league ladder as possible, but after Ten Hag's first season, he fell just short, missing out on promotion to the third division in the final minutes of the season. He was still given the benefit of the doubt, seeing as many of his squad were called up to Guardiola's first team to train with them, especially during the winter break. The likes of Pierre-Emile Højbjerg, Mitchell Weiser, Julian Green, Alessandro Schöpf and Lukas Raeder were all part of the team, but often split their time between Guardiola and Ten Hag's sides.

Raeder played under Ten Hag for just a season in the 2013/14 campaign but has positive memories of his time, as he tells me: 'He was a very professional coach right from the start. He always had his structure for trainings and his speeches or when he prepared for games. The football philosophy was very similar to Pep Guardiola's football philosophy. He wanted his team to have good passing qualities, keep the ball and always play with the ball. His teams needed to keep the ball well. That was the most important aspect.'

A goalkeeper who is now at Lokomotiv Plovdiv, Raeder was part of separate trainings, as is often the case for those in net, but recalls both Guardiola and Ten Hag asked for similar things from their keepers: mainly, being good with their feet. 'It was similar to Guardiola, but maybe not as intense. He had his plans for what he wanted from his goalkeepers. When we did tactics, most of the time, we were advised on how to switch sides and be available for the team when it's needed. I'm not sure how training was for the outfield players, but what I would hear from them was that it wasn't too much or over the top. We've heard about other coaches where trainings get exhausting, but with Ten Hag, it was not the case. However, there was still a high level of intensity, especially learning with the ball on the pitch.'

Ten Hag's second season involved a near miss too, as they won their regional championship but were still unable to get promoted, falling short to Würzburger Kickers. He would then depart Germany for FC Utrecht back home in the Netherlands, where he once played. With an established but modest club in the *Eredivisie*, he would finally have his shot in the Dutch top flight, where he would be their new manager and technical director.

Raeder looks back on that sole season working together with fondness and remembers the build-up to matches: 'We always watched one video. For me, my week was mostly spent with the first team and one day before the match I go to the second team, so I can't say if there was a lot of video analysis during the week; however, one day before the match or on matchday, he showed us some aspects of the opposition. He picked two or three important points such as if they have a strong wide winger or if their forward was to make some special movements. Then, he would explain how he would want us to play and that was how he went about in the last speech before the game.'

The goalkeeper also points out that the job was quite difficult. Ten Hag is a thorough coach, but plans were often affected by important players spending time with both the first and second team. 'Both [Guardiola and Ten Hag] want to have their success, and there was a time where it seemed difficult for Ten Hag to coach the second team. This was because the second team sometimes had to give players to the first team or some player from the first team would drop down to the second team and then he had to integrate them, possibly even just one day before a match. You could feel that there were sometimes problems with it because he'd make his plans and would want to execute it in a certain way, but that may not have always been possible.'

Despite the challenge, it was still a positive experience for Ten Hag. 'I was formed by the Dutch style, but Munich has sharpened my vision. The experience there, always wanting to win and Guardiola's dominant football, that appeals to me very much,' Ten Hag said about his time working in

Germany to Dutch outlet, NOS. He also praised Guardiola for teaching him that success doesn't only come as a result of what happens on the pitch, but off it as well. 'The mental part and the team building are very important. It's not just about the first 11, but about the entire dressing room.'

In previous years, Utrecht were too good to be threatened by the bottom of the table, but not quite good enough to challenge the upper ends and make a push for a European place. Ten Hag was brought in to change that. Once again, things were switched around: the dugouts were moved closer to the pitch, offices redesigned for greater transparency and players were given more freedom. He also moved into an apartment close to the club's stadium, and his silhouette was often visible at night when he was working. With a mid-range budget that arguably wasn't enough to compete with the *Eredivisie*'s best, Ten Hag would use his tactical acumen to get the best out of his squad and propel the club. Given a talented group that included the likes of Sébastien Haller, Richairo Živković and Nacer Barazite, amongst others, and mixing them with gifted youth academy graduates Bart Ramselaar and Giovanni Troupée, his tactical flexibility and man-management was well evident here.

Ten Hag implemented some big changes to improve the team. Willem Janssen, the team's captain who was previously an attacking midfielder, was converted into a centre-half to make way for others such as Yassin Ayoub and Sofyan Amrabat higher up the pitch. Utrecht often played with a 4-3-3 or a 4-4-2 with a diamond in midfield and it was Ayoub working in both boxes. They played down the middle, rarely using the wings and maintaining a narrower structure, with forwards Haller and Živković frequently moving wide to receive the ball if needed. The first season was a great success as Utrecht finished fifth (missing out on Europa League qualification in the play-offs), as well as runners-up in the KNVB Cup, where they lost 2-1 to Feyenoord. For a club that were quite unstable in the league, this was a positive return. He even added the Rinus Michels Award for the best coach of the season – a deserved honour.

By the next season, the expectation for Utrecht was to get better and it wasn't unreasonable to suggest that they could be the best of the rest – the team behind the big three of Ajax, PSV Eindhoven and Feyenoord – and even qualify for the Europa League. Once again, his team was organised, knowing what their roles were and deploying that in games. Transitions were quick, the football was crisp and, despite a tough start to the season, where they failed to win six of their first seven games and suffered 5-1 and 3-2 losses to Groningen and Ajax, respectively, they ensured a strong second half of the season to finish in fourth. They then overcame Heerenveen and AZ in the Europa League play-offs to qualify for the qualifying rounds for that competition.

Chris David, who knew Ten Hag since he was a child and worked with him at Utrecht, told me about the coach's attention to detail: 'He's tactically so strong. I've had lots of coaches in my career and some great ones as well and tactically, he's the best I've had. He always prepared us so well for many different situations within the game itself and focused heavily on the tactical side of football. He used to analyse opponents so well and after matches he always kept an eye on the next game so all the players knew what to do, what was coming and how to win games.'

Additionally, David highlights Ten Hag's connection to his players as a vital quality: 'He's a nice person, a family person, understood our situations and always wants to hear from us. He made efforts to speak to all the players to ensure they were happy. He knew it was difficult because he could only start 11 players every week, but when we wouldn't start, he always used to emphasise that he needed us as a squad and would remind us that we would get the chances we deserved. We could always go to his office and speak to him about things.'

Players recognised the changes he made and the results were there. They respected the cultural shift he brought in. Just like his time at Go Ahead Eagles, he had the power here to make big decisions and it paid off. In 2017/18, despite beating Valletta of Malta and Lech Poznań in the opening two qualifying rounds of the Europa League, Ten Hag's side fell agonisingly short against Zenit St Petersburg (2-0 on aggregate) and were knocked out of the competition before the group stages. Nevertheless, there were some encouraging *Eredivisie* results, namely, a 2-1 away win at Ajax, where Ten Hag's shift to a 5-3-2 and use of full-backs proved too much to handle. That would be the last of his highlights of a successful spell as Amsterdam was calling. Dutch football's brightest coach was to make his way to the Amsterdam Arena. Ten Hag had done well in his career thus far and while some doubted his appointment, it was a risk worth taking.

In the time since losing to Manchester United in Stockholm, Ajax had slightly regressed, albeit in some difficult circumstances. Key players were sold, and Peter Bosz's departure also affected them. Marcel Keizer, promoted from the youth side and asked to bring that same style of football up to the first team, was unable to do that and the job seemed too big for him. The overall melancholy around the club following the collapse of youngster Abdelhak Nouri in a preseason friendly influenced them as well.

The Amsterdammers had a difficult start to the season, being knocked out of Europe entirely in the play-off rounds. This marked the first time since 1966 that Ajax had failed to reach the competition proper of either European tournament. Not only was this a big hit on their status as a club, but it also had a huge financial impact. Later in the campaign, a defeat to FC Twente in the round of 16 of the KNVB Cup in December 2017 put an end to Keizer's tenure. The timing of this was particularly peculiar. Indeed, Ajax were having a difficult campaign, but results picked up towards Christmas: a 3-0 win against PSV and a 2-1 away success against AZ just before the cup defeat to Twente led many fans to believe that Keizer could turn things around, but the sacking made many feel that Ten Hag's appointment had been planned well in advance. The gap wasn't that big: Ajax were only five points behind PSV with half the season to play – surely that could have been turned around? Not according to the men in charge.

Keizer's sacking also led to the departure of assistant Dennis Bergkamp, who had had disagreements with Overmars in the past following the sacking of Peter Bosz as well as the technical direction of the club. He had also been there since the start of the revolution and, when you factor in that him and Overmars had known each other for so long, this exit left a sour taste. Bergkamp was a huge advocate of Keizer, but Overmars wanted to make him an assistant after Bosz left. In the end, Bergkamp won, but the victory didn't last long. Also gone was Hennie Spijkerman, associated with the first team's coaching staff since 2011, making this one of the biggest decisions of Overmars's tenure.

The risk, from Overmars's perspective, was huge. If Ten Hag failed, he failed, and the tumultuous nature of Keizer's sacking only raised the pressure. The man from Haaksbergen had plenty to win over. There often isn't a good feeling of those who join Ajax from outside Amsterdam, but recent history had shown that the most successful Ajax coaches had come from outside the city. Ronald Koeman was from Zaandam, north of Amsterdam, and he won two league titles and a cup. Bosz, from Apeldoorn, put Ajax back on the European map in his sole season in 2016/17. Ten Hag had to do something similar.

The lack of available candidates made Ten Hag an easy option and his good relationship with Overmars, who had been in contact with him since their days at Go Ahead Eagles, made him an easy choice. By Christmas, Ten Hag was ready for a new start. At the start of 2018, Edwin van der Sar's public comments about doubts over Keizer's competence as head coach caused further confusion – it was their decision to appoint him, so why were they complaining after sacking him?

Work would resume for Ten Hag, however, but he too had an unconvincing start. A loss to Vitesse in March put a dent in Ajax's title hopes and on 15 April, PSV could claim the title with a win in Amsterdam over Ajax. The Eindhoven club trounced them 3-0 and that caused rage amongst the fans, who stopped the team bus after the loss, demanding an explanation as to why they hadn't won a league title since 2014.

The fans were livid, and so was the media. Keizer was the man that stuck with Ajax as a youth coach, promoted key players over the years and was there when Ajax suffered one of the most traumatic experiences in recent times – the collapse of the beloved Nouri. Ten Hag had a lot to do to make up for that but there was little optimism that he could. Overmars and Van der Sar, however, thought differently and were hoping the risk would pay off in the 2018/19 season.

The core of the side was great: André Onana had great potential, Matthijs de Ligt was a future star, a midfield consisting of Donny van de Beek and Frenkie de Jong was something to cherish, while in attack, David Neres and Hakim Ziyech had magic. The best part was that they were all young, and improving youngsters was Ten Hag's expertise. He just needed the time and support, and that's what he got. Many were still pessimistic. Maybe Ajax should've looked abroad. Maybe this generation of fine talents would be wasted. But Ajax stuck with their man. Stubborn but with an unprecedented work ethic, demanding but with an incredible emotional awareness, this is Ten Hag, *De Tukker*, the man charged with helping Ajax return to the top.

MARC OVERMARS'S BELLY FLOP

Remembering the most beautiful
season in Ajax's recent history

i: THE EXPERT

In a Champions League round of 16 match against Inter in 2006, Klaas-Jan Huntelaar scored a towering header – his first goal in the competition – to give Ajax the lead. The match finished 2-2 and the Dutch forward, then only 22, described this as one of the more satisfying goals of his early career to *Voetbal International*: 'The one against Inter had a certain charge, because it was a top match. I was curious how I would hold up against a top defender like Walter Samuel. It went well. Before I scored he tried to block me, but I saw him coming out of the corner of my eye and I pushed him instead of him pushing me. Those are instructive moments and a confirmation that I can also hold my own at that level.' That would be his only goal in the Champions League for Ajax.

Huntelaar was born in Voor-Drempt, near Doetinchem, some 120km from Amsterdam. He wasn't born or bred close to Ajax – playing for the likes of De Graafschap and Go Ahead Eagles when he was younger – but had the club in his heart, despite his career starting off at rivals PSV

Eindhoven. The forward's time at PSV was hardly fruitful, but he shone at Heerenveen, which earned him a move to his beloved Ajax in the winter of 2006. This was a different Ajax to the one he grew up supporting. Huntelaar watched the teams of Louis van Gaal in the 1990s, but now it was a side struggling to cope with modern football. Still, he did his best and succeeded. The goal against Inter was one of 105 he scored for Ajax and in January 2009 he left for Real Madrid for a fee rising to €27m – about three times of what he signed for three years ago.

Like he loved Ajax, the fans loved him back. Two KNVB Cup successes and some iconic performances were some of the highlights, but the tenure felt incomplete. The Real Madrid spell didn't go as planned, neither did his time at Milan in Italy and it was in Germany with Schalke where he would find his feet again. In 2017, after seven glorious years in Gelsenkirchen with memories aplenty, he would return to Ajax. Now, Huntelaar was older, wiser, with different ambitions. He wasn't the up-and-coming forward looking to make his mark in the game. He already had a legacy in football and in Amsterdam. The first season back, like it was for the club as a whole, was a roller coaster which had two coaches in Marcel Keizer and Erik ten Hag, but in 2018/19, Huntelaar would prove his importance once again.

The team was ambitious. Kasper Dolberg had earned himself a positive reputation in previous years, while Ajax also spent big on reinforcing the attacking line with the signing of Dušan Tadić, in addition to Hakim Ziyech and David Neres who were already there. There wasn't a guarantee that Huntelaar would be given time on the field, so he had to make every chance count – and he did. Never before had Ajax started a season as early as they did in

2018/19. It was 25 July when they first kicked a ball in a competitive match that season. Having finished as runners-up in the *Eredivisie* in the previous campaign, Ajax would have to go through three rounds of two legs each to make it to the competition proper of the Champions League, and the first obstacle on the way there was Sturm Graz, just ten days after that year's World Cup Final in Russia.

Fortunately for Ajax, most of their players were fresh and didn't need resting after the World Cup, but pressure to win was huge: qualifying for the group stages of the Champions League, something they hadn't done since 2014, was of paramount importance. From a financial perspective, the Champions League had slipped further away from Europe's non-top five leagues. UEFA's top four in the coefficient rankings, England, Spain, Italy and Germany, were guaranteed four spots in the group stages – half of the 32 that make up the competition proper – leaving just 16 spots for the rest of Europe and a smaller prize pool to claim from. PSV, the Dutch champions, had to go through a qualification process too, albeit a smaller one. Getting to the group stage had its own perks: a €14.5m fee guaranteed and then add-ons for performances: €2.7 million for a win and €900,000 for a draw in the group stage.

With six Champions League and European Cup winners, the Netherlands are the fifth-most successful country in the competition's history, but Ajax in 1995 were its last winners. That was reflected in the uneven income distribution. According to data by Consultancy.nl, between 2003 and 2017, Dutch teams earned a total of €364m from their Champions League participation, with Ajax earning €135m, behind PSV's €198.2m. English clubs earned the most (€2.18b), followed by Spain (€1.88b), Italy (€1.59b),

Germany (€1 .43b) and France (€1.16b). The odds are often stacked against Dutch clubs, making qualification to the group stage vital. For the 2018/19 season, there was a bigger pool – over €1.9b was available to be distributed amongst participating clubs, and Ajax wanted a chunk.

The Johan Cruyff Arena, as it was now known as a tribute to the late great Ajax hero, was buzzing for the return of the Champions League, but they were cautious. Ajax had been here before and fallen. The year before it was Nice from France and prior to that, Rostov and Rapid Wien got the better of them. However, Ziyech calmed nerves early on – his meagre shot was fumbled to give Ajax the lead and the Moroccan waltzed away in his telephone celebration, a popular sight in Amsterdam. Early in the second half, Lasse Schöne, the embodiment of calmness, added a second, getting in on the rebound after his penalty was saved. Ajax were up by two, and the fans were jubilant. A week later, they had to finish the job in Austria.

At the Mercuur Arena in Graz, Ajax were in a good position, and Huntelaar capitalised. In the 39th minute, he brought down Neres's cross and put it into the bottom right of the net to score his second Champions League goal for Ajax. He would add another towards the end of the game, receiving a pass from Maximilian Wöber – that was Ajax's third. In the middle, Tadić scored his first goal for the club and even a bizarre André Onana own goal right at the death didn't dampen spirits. Ajax were through.

Standard Liège of Belgium awaited them, and this was a side Ajax had history with. Just two years prior, Peter Bosz took his Ajax side to Liège in the Europa League and the scenes amongst the fans got ugly. Here they were, under Ten Hag, with a much more mature side: the likes of Frenkie de

Jong, Matthijs de Ligt and Donny van de Beek had grown. Standard had the upper hand early on in the first leg at home, but Ajax drew first blood: once again, Huntelaar struck with a fine diving header from a Tadić cross. In the little time the pair spent together, they were forming a fine partnership. The Serbian then got on the scoresheet again and by half-time they were 2-0 up and cruising. By full time, things weren't quite the same: two goals by Standard Liège, including a 94th-minute penalty, raised doubts – maybe, once again, Ajax would suffer Champions League disappointment?

In the second leg, Ten Hag's side erased any lingering questions. Huntelaar, who was becoming a frequent name on the scoresheet early in the season, opened the scoring (albeit, it should've been ruled out for offside), netting his fourth goal in the qualifying rounds, and his goal was added to by De Ligt from a corner and Neres with a tap-in. Ajax had the away goals advantage coming into the tie, but they weren't taking any chances. A complete performance, rounded off by three well-taken goals, wrapped up a deserved victory and another jump over a hurdle on their way to Champions League qualification. Now, just one team stood between Ajax and the group stage.

It's 22 August 2018. Ajax are playing Dynamo Kyiv and the Champions League group stage draw is a little over a week away, and Ajax want to be in it. Before the game against the Ukrainians, Ten Hag talks about making the Johan Cruyff Arena a fortress, about not being scared of opponents if they want to play against the best and using this tie to set a precedent for the future. On the pitch, the players listened. Within 80 seconds, Van de Beek struck and the stadium was joyous. That pride didn't last long, however. A few minutes later, De Ligt lost his man at a corner and even though Onana made a save, the rebound fell to Tomasz Kędziora, who struck into an empty net. Ajax weren't deterred. Soon, Ziyech, on the wing, cut inside and hit a fierce strike that found its way in with help from a deflection – 2-1 Ajax. Then, Tadić, quickly becoming a fan favourite, met a cross from Nicolás Tagliafico from the left. 3-1 in the first-half, and Ajax held on.

The return leg was tense: Dynamo Kyiv had the away goal. Ajax advised fans not to travel to Ukraine due to hooliganism fears, meaning the home side had an added advantage. And if there was enough tension amongst fans before kick-off, the start to the game only made it worse, especially early on. Onana was forced into a significant early save, the reliable Tadić missed a penalty with his shot hitting the post, Van de Beek narrowly missed a chance to add to Ajax's lead, Denys Boyko in the Dynamo Kyiv net made crucial saves from Huntelaar and Noussair Mazraoui and Ziyech's free kick also hit the woodwork. It was anywhere but the net for Ajax, but it was enough. The tie could've flipped anywhere at any time, but it didn't and there they were, jubilant in celebration after making it to the Champions League group stages for the first time in six years. For Ten Hag, the job became slightly easier, and he needed this win more than anyone.

Post-match, the reaction from the players was identical. De Jong said it was his first time in the group stages and that was the case for many others in the team. Van de Beek and Daley Blind, back from Manchester United that summer, said it had been too long without proper Champions League football. Ten Hag praised his team's set-up and unity.

Domestically, things were improving too and Huntelaar was at the heart of it. While the qualification rounds were ongoing, in the *Eredivisie*, the 35-year-old was firing: two goals against Emmen and Vitesse either side of the matches against Dynamo Kyiv and then one against Groningen after September's international break proved his value to the team. He was needed and, even though this was a different Ajax, the experience was necessary and Huntelaar brought just that. The boy from Voor-Drempt loved Ajax – he starred for them when he was younger, then travelled Europe, came back, and was just as loved. Now, even though he wasn't guaranteed a place in the first team, he wanted to show he still had it, and he did so successfully.

ii: 'BARCELONA OR MANCHESTER CITY?'

In 2017, after Ajax's Europa League semi-final win over Lyon, a 17-year-old Matthijs de Ligt went over to the travelling Ajax support sat in the away end of the Parc Olympique Lyonnais. Ajax had reached their first European final in 21 years. De Ligt, wearing number 36, a number normally associated with emerging youth players like him, went over to thank the fans, who went through a roller coaster of emotions that evening. He led them into a famous chant, usually sung by supporters' groups F-side and VAK410.

De Ligt: '*Wonen daar ook Superjoden?*' (Do Super Jews live there too?)

Supporters: '*Ja daar wonen Superjoden!*' (Yes, there are Super Jews!)

De Ligt: '*Vinden Joden voetbal fijn?*' (Do Jews like football?)

Supporters: '*Als ze maar voor Ajax zijn!*' (As long as they support Ajax!)

Both: '*Amsterdam, Amsterdam, Amsterdam!*'

It was brief, but it told plenty about him. As the video went viral, fans from around the world praised the defender for his level-headedness throughout the tournament, including the final, where he was arguably Ajax's best player despite their defeat to Manchester United, and cited him as a future captain of the club. Fast forward two years, and he was indeed their captain. De Ligt, now 19 and wearing number 4, a number more associated with first-team players, was leading this young Ajax side into the Champions League and he held the armband ahead of some of the more experienced members of the side, including Daley Blind. The teenager was seen as the model professional and an example of what a De Toekomst graduate should be like.

De Ligt, who previously favoured tennis over football, joined Ajax as a nine-year-old boy, despite concerns over his physique, but it was his ball-playing abilities that won scouts over. At 15, he found his place in defence, having previously played in midfield. Influenced at the club by Jaap Stam and Frank de Boer, who were there amongst the coaching staff when De Ligt was growing up, he had the right people around him to help him improve as a footballer. His growth was rapid, playing in age groups above his age and constantly progressing, and it came as no surprise to those at the club that he was playing in a continental final at 17, in his first season in professional football.

'It's really nice,' he once told CNN about his relationship with the club's supporters. 'I was a fan before when I was younger, so I watched a lot of games and I was always singing in the crowd and shouting when the referee made a mistake or something, you know? And now to play in the Arena, to be captain of this team, is something else, a dream … I dreamed of becoming Ajax captain, but more like at the age of 24 or 25, to be honest. That it came so soon is really special.'

In Ajax's return to the Champions League, they were placed in a group alongside Bayern Munich, Benfica and AEK Athens. The biggest challenge of them was, of course, the German record champions, coach Erik ten Hag's former club, where he worked between 2013 and 2015. After the completion of the draw, Ten Hag revealed he received a text from compatriot and Bayern winger Arjen Robben – they were both looking forward to the tie but would have to wait. First, there was a game against AEK Athens in Amsterdam, which was Ajax's first group stage game in the Champions League since 11 December 2014 – 1,378 days ago.

De Ligt, who was on the verge of history, would have to sit this game out. He suffered an injury in the build-up to the match and was doubtful for the league match against PSV Eindhoven at the weekend as well. On the pitch, he was hardly missed. Ajax were on top throughout as they asserted their dominance over their Greek opponents. Nicolás Tagliafico, the Argentine left-back who had only joined earlier in 2018 from Independiente, had quickly become a favourite for his tenacity, and he scored twice, the second of which was an intended cross that found its way into the net. Chants of 'Nicooo! Nicooo!' rung around the stadium and there were plenty of Argentinian flags evident. Sandwiched in between the full-back's two goals was one from Donny van de Beek, who started the game on the bench. Ajax, on their return to the Champions League, won 3-0 and the Arena was elated.

The joy was short-lived, though. Just four days later, against PSV, a confusing team selection saw Daley Blind pair up with Frenkie de Jong at centre-half to make up for the injured De Ligt and bad memories returned again. PSV won 3-0 – the same scoreline by which the Eindhoven side beat Ajax a few months prior to win the league title. Although no championship was decided in this September fixture, it didn't help clear the doubts about Ten Hag, whose start at Ajax was bumpy at best. 'Painful. Frustrating. You just can't believe what happened in that first half. One goal, two goals, three goals. We were giving them away. It felt like the ground was sinking under out feet,' Tadić said.

The response to the defeat against PSV was positive. Ajax went on an 11-game winning streak in the *Eredivisie*, lasting all the way until the winter break and making positive strides in the chase for a first title since 2014. In Europe, attentions turned to the away trip to Bayern Munich, Ajax's biggest test in the Champions League so far. With De Jong now injured, Van de Beek started in midfield. In defence, Max Wöber made a return with Blind pushed into defensive midfield while De Ligt finally made his Champions League debut, becoming the second-youngest captain in the competition's history, behind Rúben Neves when he was at Porto. Up top, Tadić led the line himself, as he would do for much of the club's European campaign.

The start was hardly ideal: Mats Hummels scored in the fourth minute from an easy header, but it was the jolt Ajax needed. From there, it was total control from the visitors, and they got a quick reward – Tadić set up right-back Noussair Mazraoui for the equaliser. After that, they had three big chances to net a second, with Tadić, Tagliafico and Van de Beek all missing and Lasse Schöne's free kick hitting the bar. Ajax were brave, they dared to play and proved they could cut it amongst Europe's elite. A point was a fair reward, and they left the Allianz Arena with their heads held high. Post-match, Hakim Ziyech, stood beside Louis van Gaal, who awkwardly glared at him while the Moroccan spoke to Dutch television, praised the team spirit. Ziyech received plaudits from the German media as well. They labelled him a *zauberer* – a wizard – for his creativity in attack.

Their third tie was home to Benfica, where Ajax would don their black, white and beige away kit due to a kit clash. That kit would go on to become synonymous with this team that season. Like the game against Bayern, this too was stern. Benfica's Haris Seferovic had the first real chance, but his shot was cleared off the line by De Ligt, and in a game of half chances for both sides, it took until the end for the winner to be found. In the 92nd minute, Ajax drove forward with David Neres, who came on as a substitute, and his cross towards Kasper Dolberg was cleared away only to fall to Mazraoui, who released a shot that went in via a deflection. Ajax had won at the death; it was Mazraoui who scored again and sealed an important win. The Dutch side had seven points from their first three Champions League games, their top scorers were their two full-backs and they believed that for the first time in 13 years they could qualify for the knockout rounds.

Ajax were freely scoring goals and growing in confidence. The quality they showed on the European stage was now reciprocated in the domestic competitions as well. Losing to PSV brought some gloom, but they recovered well from it, as evident in a dominant 5-0 win over AZ and a 3-0 *Klassiker* success over Feyenoord. They wanted to end that title drought. There was only a tiny problem: while Ajax were doing well, PSV were doing even better. Their Champions League group was a tough task, featuring

Barcelona, Inter and Tottenham, but domestically, they were almost perfect.

In the Champions League, with qualification so close, Ajax drew 1-1 with Benfica with Tadić scoring again from a tight angle. It was a valuable point on their path and they could confirm their entry into the last 16 with a win over AEK Athens with a game to spare. Ajax recognised the challenge Bayern could pose them, so they picked up essential points against the rest.

In the international break, De Ligt reaffirmed his commitment to Ajax. Having impressed so much over the years, rumours swirled around Europe about interest in the defender. He was still a teenager, and every top club wanted him. After a Nations League match against France, he was asked directly: 'Which is the nicer club: Manchester City or Barcelona?' De Ligt's response was simple: 'Ajax.' There was a growing feeling that these were his last few months at the club, but to hear that he was fully backing Ajax to have a good season was reassuring. He had been at the club since he was a boy, and he only wanted to leave when it was in a good place. Back in Europe, another pair of goals from Tadić against AEK Athens in an eerie Greek atmosphere marred by crowd trouble confirmed Ajax's qualification. They reached the last 16 for the first time since the 2005/06 season; De Ligt became the first Ajax captain to lead them this far since Tomáš Galásek and, financially, there was more coming into the bank.

With only top spot in the group to contend in the final group game against Bayern Munich, Ajax brought their mojo again, and the game was a treat. Both teams went down to ten men with Wöber and Thomas Müller sent off, but the match wasn't as unfriendly as it may seem. Robert

Lewandowski put Bayern in front, but Ajax hit back with another Tadić double. Lewandowski then got a second from a penalty of his own, before Kingsley Coman and Tagliafico scored one each to end the game at 3-3.

It was a thriller at the Arena and although Ajax didn't win their group, falling two points short of the Bavarians, they felt they could take on any team. Now, Europe was taking notice: this Ajax team were something serious. They were unbeaten throughout the group stage – three wins and three draws – and Ten Hag recognised the room for improvement: 'We must learn from our mistakes from these games, including tonight's match,' he said after the Bayern draw. 'But, most certainly, we have realised we can play at this level. We are a real competitor and I think no opponent would be happy to face Ajax.'

iii: THE NUMBER 10

There was surprise around Dušan Tadić suddenly rising to become one of the Champions League's top players after the group stage of the 2018/19 campaign. It mainly came from England where Tadić was a solid, if not spectacular, Premier League footballer for Southampton between 2014 and 2018. His strengths were known: people knew what he could bring to the team and knew he was a threat, but at Ajax this was a different Tadić to the one they were used to seeing. Tadić's move to Ajax in itself came as a bit of a surprise. He had offers from several clubs abroad in 2018, including a Chinese side – believed to be Dalian Yifang – who offered him a €42m, three-season contract to move there. He refused. Ajax was his boyhood dream.

'From a young age I've always loved Ajax,' Tadić once said to *The Guardian*. 'A lot of clubs were really interested but I said to Southampton that I only wanted to go to Ajax. Perhaps they wanted me to go to another club, but I was immediately clear. I said: "This is the only club that I want to go to.'"

The *Eredivisie* was a swaying factor too – Tadić admitted the physicality of the Premier League was a bit much and that the Dutch top flight would enable him to prolong his playing career. He also previously had a good time in the league, playing for Groningen for two years between 2010 and 2012 before joining FC Twente, also for two years between 2012 and 2014, scoring 42 goals across the four seasons.

The spell at Southampton propelled Tadić to greater heights. Under former Ajax manager Ronald Koeman, they carried the Saints to their finest-ever Premier League campaign in 2014/15 and he was widely respected on the south coast of England. The opportunity to join Ajax was too good to ignore and, after the World Cup in Russia, the deal was complete: €11.4m up front in a deal that could rise to €13.7m in performance-related bonuses – just short of being the club's most expensive footballer ever. It was still a big purchase, and an indication of the 'new Ajax'. Tadić was too old to have a big resale value if he was to leave in the future, but young enough to be considered as a player who was in the final years of his career.

Upon joining, the Serbian requested to wear the number 10 shirt, then occupied by Hakim Ziyech. The request was obliged. Ziyech wasn't expected to be at the club by the end of the 2018 transfer window. In previous months, his relations with Ajax weren't the best, and he was going through a difficult period himself. The collapse of Abdelhak Nouri a year prior still affected him, and when he was named as Ajax's Player of the Season for 2017/18, there was a sense of reluctant happiness: the club didn't have a good season and he had a souring rapport with the fans. In February 2018, they were booing him at the Amsterdam Arena. In April 2018, after PSV won the league title in Amsterdam and fans stormed the Ajax bus, Ziyech was hassled by a supporter, which led to the deletion of many photos on his personal Instagram account. That felt as though it was his last act. To see him wear the red and white of Ajax in 2018/19 would be a surprise.

But his and Morocco's underwhelming performances at the World Cup meant that the right offer didn't arrive, and there he was, back at Ajax, ready for another season. His number 10 had gone to the new signing, and he took up the number 22. While there were whispers that the two wouldn't get along, on the pitch they squashed those doubts almost immediately – complementing each other perfectly. Off it, they built a strong connection: Tadić quickly became a popular figure in the dressing room, and he managed to convince Ziyech to prolong his Amsterdam stay.

With the group stage wrapped up in fine fashion, Ajax were confident. In the draw, they got Real Madrid, the side that had won the tournament three times on the bounce and had the reigning Ballon d'Or holder, Luka Modrić. This was a different Real Madrid, though. After beating Liverpool in the previous season's final, coach Zinedine Zidane departed and, a while later, Cristiano Ronaldo, the club's greatest goalscorer, made his way to Juventus. Julen Lopetegui was Zidane's replacement, but he was sacked after a weak start that culminated in a 5-1 defeat to Barcelona at the Camp Nou. Santiago Solari, the former Argentine winger who was managing *Los Blaneos*'s youth sides, was his replacement until the end of the season, and when the draw was made, Ajax felt this was a winnable tie. They were improving, while Real Madrid looked uncertain and out of sorts.

But still, this was Real Madrid. They still had more talent within their squad than Ajax. They still had more experience in their squad than Ajax. They still had more Champions League know-how than Ajax. Real Madrid, the 13-time champions, were no pushovers. Ajax's own recent history with the Spanish side didn't paint a pretty picture: under Frank de Boer, they faced Real Madrid six times across three successive seasons in the group stages and lost all the matches, scoring just two goals and conceding 20. Additionally, it was also a Real Madrid defeat of Ajax in the Champions League that inspired Johan Cruyff's first column in *De Telegraaf*, which laid the foundations for the Velvet Revolution.

Going into the tie against Real Madrid, Ajax had a problem in their domestic run. Their post-Christmas form took a slump: a 4-4 draw against Heerenveen despite having a 3-1 lead at one point, a 1-0 loss to Heracles and a 6-2 battering at Feyenoord set them back in the title race. After the defeat to Heracles, they were six points behind PSV and had already dropped more points in the league as well as conceded more goals in the four matches after the winter break than they did in the 17 before it.

They needed to pick up quickly, and they did so against Solari's side. In the first leg at the Johan Cruyff Arena, Ajax started off brilliantly, matching their opponents in terms of intensity, and they picked up an early goal through Nicolás Tagliafico, who pounced on a rebound, but that was ruled out by the Video Assistant Referee – the first time ever that VAR had overturned a Champions League goal.

The frustration was added to in the second half: Karim Benzema, often Ajax's nemesis, scored the opener with a fine finish in the box. However, 15 minutes after conceding, the Tadić and Ziyech combination worked again, with the Moroccan netting the equaliser. 1-1 would've been a fair result, but football often isn't fair. Just before the end, Marco Asensio got on the end of a cross from Dani Carvajal. Real Madrid led and won 2-1. Towards the end, Sergio Ramos intentionally got booked to miss the second leg and keep a clean record ahead of a potential quarter-final. He'd done this once before against Ajax – in 2010 – and he did it here again.

In previous ties against Real Madrid, Ajax were often taken apart, but they held their own here. 2-1 ideally wouldn't have been a bad result – if anything, it was quite honourable, and they still had a chance to pull off a miracle – but the overall context and the last few weeks where their domestic season was stuttering made it tough to take. Ahead of the second leg in Madrid, things were better. Two successive league wins kept them in the title hunt, and a KNVB Cup semi-final success over Feyenoord at De Kuip brought some reprieve to the 6-2 loss exactly a month ago. Ahead of the match at the Santiago Bernabéu, there were dreams aplenty. It was unlikely, but it could've been magical if matters went to plan. Ajax memories were clouded by the group stage disappointments under De Boer, but they were hoping for more 1995 than 2010s, when they famously beat Real Madrid at their home and left with an applause.

Like the first leg at home, coach Erik ten Hag sent out the team that suited Tadić's strengths. The 'Tadić variant', where the Serb was the roaming forward, supported by Ziyech and David Neres on the wings with Frenkie de Jong, Lasse Schöne and Donny van de Beek behind him, was sent out on to the pitch in Madrid.

It took just seven minutes for the nerves to set in. There was trouble brewing, but not for Ajax. Tadić drove forward from the right wing, a goalscoring opportunity, and he found his partner in crime, Ziyech, who stylishly finished past Thibaut Courtois in the Real Madrid net. 1-0 Ajax, and it didn't stop there. Minute 19, and it was that magician again, the one with the 10 on his back. He moved forward and performed a beautiful roulette, or a *Zidaantje* (Zidane turn) as it's called in the Netherlands, past Casemiro. The audience was stunned – Tadić made it look so easy, and he set up Neres. A step past Courtois, open net, and he scores. 2-0 Ajax. The advantage is with the visitors – they led 3-2 on aggregate. Luck was on their side too. Bale, who had come on as a substitute, hit the post. Vinícius Jr and Vázquez went off injured and Varane hit the woodwork early on.

In the second half, Tadić got in on the act himself, and this was the perfect Ajax goal. Mazroaoui won it in his half and the team flowed forward like a cool breeze. Tagliafico, Ziyech, Van de Beek, all involved before Tadić's wonderful finish from outside the box. This was Ajax at their very best. They played sumptuous football not just with the ball but without it too. Tadić was at the centre of it all. This was the ex-Southampton man that nobody recognised and he was the orchestrator at the Bernabéu. Asensio managed to make it 3-1, but even that was cancelled out by Schöne's stunning free kick soon after. It was 4-1 at the end, 5-3 on aggregate, and the back-to-back-to-back European champions were sent packing. The Dutch side were through to the quarter-finals of the Champions League for the first time since 2003, and they didn't rely on a moment or a debatable refereeing decision, they beat Real Madrid in style, in the only style they knew.

Ten Hag, the master, was full of praise, and didn't want to stop. Speaking after the victory: 'It's been a long time since a Dutch team has shown this in Europe. The big money in the big leagues has become more and more decisive in recent decades. For a small football country it is difficult to compete with that. We are doing that now. We are on a wonderful journey and I would like it to continue for a while. Today we crossed another boundary. Where is the ceiling? No idea, but we want more.'

At the age of 30, Tadić had the match of his life. French daily *L'Équipe* who had only given a perfect ten out of ten in their player ratings nine times previously added a tenth – it was Tadić. The Serb was the first player since 1997 to get a ten without scoring four goals in a game. Before him, the likes of Lionel Messi, Robert Lewandowski and Neymar all had to bag a quartet to get there.

At the Real Madrid end, captain Ramos, sat in the VIP box having missed the game through suspension, was filming a documentary about his life but his filming crew packed up as Real Madrid were being embarrassed on the pitch. The next morning, the press didn't hold back. *Marca* called it a 'humiliating end' to their Champions League dominance. *Sport* said it was the 'end of an era'. *AS* called it a 'tragic week' as Real Madrid's season was rendered pointless. Catalan paper *Mundo Deportivo* said was full of praise for the victors: 'A huge Ajax gives a football recital and causes an earthquake [in Madrid] with unpredictable consequences.'

Ajax were through. Amsterdam, and large parts of Europe, were jubilant. Maybe it was great to see the return of a fallen giant. Maybe it was the way in which they did it. Maybe it was because the same team wouldn't win the

Champions League for a fourth year in a row. Whatever it was, there was a general satisfaction to witness that Ajax win. For the neutrals, it was a fine evening of football, but for those so closely linked with Ajax, it was a dream. Hank Spaan, writing in *Het Parool* the day after the match, put it best: 'People were asking and wondering in droves if they had been dreaming at times. At some point I put the phone away. Alone in the dark, only by the light of the [television] screen, I retreated into a match that was reality while seeming to be built from dream images. You don't want to overdo it by adding something intangible like luck. But that match yesterday was a ninety-minute trek into the intangible.'

iv: SERENE GENIUS

Amidst the enchantment of the match at the Santiago Bernabéu, a famous Ajax image was born. It came from Frenkie de Jong getting the ball and quickly dribbling past Luka Modrić, using both his feet and leaving the Croat on his backside. It felt like a changing of the guard, like the world's best midfielder handing the crown over to the future. The picture, captured by Etsuo Hara for Getty Images, became a symbol of that famed Ajax win. In the morning after the match, *El País* suggested that Real Madrid 'bathed in reality', and this image perhaps encapsulated that. De Jong was an exquisite midfielder, making complex actions look incredibly mundane. He was in his final few months at Ajax and he made sure he and the club enjoyed it.

Born in the Dutch village of Arkel and named after the band Frankie Goes to Hollywood, albeit with a Dutch twist, De Jong, like most Dutch footballers, dreamed of playing for Barcelona. The Catalan club were popular in the Netherlands, largely because of Johan Cruyff and the *Barçajax* connection, and De Jong was no different to many other kids in the Netherlands – the *Blaugrana* meant prestige. When his move to Barcelona was confirmed in January 2019, De Jong's girlfriend, Mikky Kiemeney, posted a picture from 2015 – when De Jong was 18 – on her Instagram account of the two visiting the Camp Nou. His love for Barça was real and everlasting, and it wouldn't be long before his dreams would become reality.

De Jong's career started off at Willem II and he made his debut for the senior team in January 2015. His talent was identified from a young age and the country's two top clubs kept eyes on him from the start: both PSV and Ajax wanted him, and it was the latter that won the race. The deal was secured in the summer, and he stayed on loan until the end of the year before joining Jong Ajax. There was so much faith in his talent that Ajax agreed for a transfer of just €1, with a sell-on clause of ten per cent for any future transfer. De Jong had broken through with the senior Ajax set-up by 2016, but it wasn't until two years later, in 2018, that he really became one of their standout stars.

That year, after the World Cup and with the appointment of Ronald Koeman as the Netherlands head coach, the Dutch were looking to build a new era. They failed to qualify for Euro 2016 as well as the World Cup in 2018 but had optimism for the future, and Koeman saw De Jong as the centrepiece of his *Oranje* midfield. That September, the first international break after the World Cup, they faced France in Paris in the Nations League, and De Jong stood out. France won 2-1, but De Jong was the best player on the pitch. The youngster was at ease throughout, swaying through and playing like he had been on this stage forever, even though it was his first start for his country.

The following weeks were complicated by injury and a spell of playing in defence, but when France visited the Netherlands for the return fixture, De Jong was at it again. This was his breakthrough game and it ended with a Dutch win. Three days after that, they drew against Germany, and there was overall praise aimed at De Jong. He backed that up with stellar performances for Ajax, adding in an unusual string of goals, as Erik ten Hag also discovered his best team. De Jong wasn't a centre-half – for him to be at his best, he needed to be in midfield. That phase between September and December was him showing his qualities, and when the January transfer window rolled around, there was interest in him from the finest in Europe. Manchester City, Paris Saint-Germain and his dream club, Barcelona, all wanted him and, at one point, it seemed as though he was leaning towards the French side.

However, he was convinced to move to Catalonia. A fee of €75m was agreed and De Jong would move to La Liga in the summer. According to the *Financial Times*, then Barça president Josep Maria Bartomeu concluded the negotiations by convincing De Jong he was in for a special time at Barcelona: 'If you look for a coach, go with Pep Guardiola, but when he will leave City, I don't know who is going to be the following coach,' Bartomeu said. 'If you look for money, go to PSG. You will be a billionaire. But, if you want to enjoy your life for the next 12, 14 years, come to Barcelona.' The deal was done, and De Jong was to spend six months in Amsterdam.

It made the win over Real Madrid even more special – now, even the Barcelona fans had a deep connection to it. Their future midfielder had ended the Madrid club's hold of the trophy, and De Jong had a huge role in it. If Dušan Tadić was the head chef of that special night, De Jong was the maître d', conducting his team and controlling proceedings. The image with Modrić staring into the camera in bemusement became iconic and Ajax were ready for more.

In the pot for the quarter-final draw along with Ajax were a host of big names: four English clubs including Manchester City and Liverpool, who were having a title race for the ages, were involved, as well as Barcelona, where Lionel Messi was enjoying another stellar campaign, and Juventus, who were ultimately paired with Ajax. The summer prior, they had signed Cristiano Ronaldo, making him their most expensive footballer ever. Ronaldo had priors against Ajax – he was the architect of their downfall whenever he faced them with Real Madrid, and from a Juventus perspective, Ajax were probably the team they wanted most.

Once again, though, there would be a wait before the Juventus tie and a few games in the league, and this was where Ajax's hopes of regaining the league title would really go up, albeit with a bump at first. Against AZ, they lost 1-0 and they were played apart and, once again, they were five points behind PSV, who were their next opponents. Failure to win would effectively end their title hopes and although a win wouldn't take them to the top, it would put them in a better position. They made a fine start: an own goal from Daniel Schwaab gave Ajax the lead, but the second half put things in doubt again. Noussair Mazroaui was sent off and within a minute, an error from André Onana levelled the scores. Ajax's title hopes were dwindling away. PSV were threatening, but then, Ajax got lucky: David Neres was fouled in the box and up stepped Dušan Tadić for arguably the most critical kick of his Ajax career thus far. He scored and, at the death, Neres made it 3-1. It was one of Ajax's most important wins of the season.

That gave them the motivation for the rest of the campaign: if they were able to beat the reigning champions in those circumstances, they could take on anyone. Emmen and Willem II were comfortably put aside in the next two fixtures and, a day after the win against Willem II, PSV dropped points in a draw against Vitesse. Ajax, for the first time since May 2016, were top of the league on goal difference and this was the ideal scenario to be in before Juventus were to visit.

A repeat of the 1996 final, which was won by Juventus and raised doubts amongst figures at Ajax about doping within the camp of the Turin club, this was a chance to set the record straight, but they knew the odds were against them, especially after the first leg. After a tense first half, Ronaldo, Ajax's perennial menace, struck just towards the end of it. However, early in the second half, Neres, from a shot with his weaker right foot, got the equaliser. Ajax went to Turin with the scores level, but Juventus had the away-goal advantage and Ronaldo, who was in top form in the previous round having scored a hat-trick against Atlético Madrid, felt like he could put Ajax to the sword again.

A week later in Italy there were changes aplenty. Mazraoui, who missed the first leg, was back, this time at left-back, while Joël Veltman, having seen his role diminish under Ten Hag, was on the right. In midfield, De Jong, who had a fine first leg in Amsterdam before suffering a hamstring injury in the league, was a doubt, but he started too. Early on, Mazraoui had to go off due to injury, and

Daley Sinkgraven, another of Ajax's second-choice squad, was on. Suddenly, without their two primary full-backs, this challenge intensified. Soon after, the inevitable happened: Ronaldo scored, once again from a header having made space for himself from a corner. It was 1-0 to Juventus, home support behind them, aggregate lead, and Ajax were on the verge.

They didn't lie down, though. They were raised that way. This was the new Ajax: fearless, carefree, playing like they had nothing to lose and with the spirit of old that made them so great. They were behind for just six minutes. Hakim Ziyech's mishit shot fell perfectly to Donny van de Beek, who passed the ball into the net. It needed a stroke of luck – Juventus thought he was offside and maybe Van de Beek did too, but it stood.

Ajax were level in the tie again and then they played as though they were the favourites. The second goal, the winning goal, seemed like a matter of when, not if. Ziyech had a fine chance – so did Van de Beek for his second, but they were both saved. It took until minute 67: Matthijs de Ligt, the prized Ajax defender with a gleaming reputation, rose above all and charged at the ball. It was 2-1 in Turin; Ajax were in front and on the way to a Champions League semi-final. If one thought Juventus would come back at them, they were wrong. It was all Ajax, with Neres nearly making it 3-1. This night was as historic as the previous round – Ajax had knocked out one of the favourites.

Post-match, the reaction and praise were in full flow again: 'Incredible, incredible,' said *De Telegraaf* the morning after the win. 'The achievement did not come easily but it was deserved one hundred percent.' *De Volksrant* added: 'It was unbelievable. Ajax knocked Cristiano Ronaldo, a bystander, out of the tournament, the king of the Champions League who had been brought to Turin to win the cup here too.' In Italy, *Corriere dello Sport* were shocked: *'Apocalisse,'* they said. *Gazetta dello Sport* had a similar reaction, saying Juventus had played 'half a metre below the expected level' and they received a lesson from 'baby Ajax'. De Ligt was a star; De Jong, injured before the game, was in serene form; Daley Blind, the experienced head, showed his wisdom.

Marc Overmars, usually a quiet and reserved figure, was jubilant too. After the win, the 2,100 Ajax fans stayed behind in the Juventus Stadium, waiting to go out, when they were visited by Overmars and Edwin van der Sar, walking towards them from the dugout. The pair, who had endured so much with Ajax over the years, were delighted to see Ajax make it to their first Champions League semi-final since 1996. They walked towards the supporters, Van der Sar was shouting and pumping his fists while Overmars took off his jacket, ran towards the supporters and performed a belly flop – a nod to his former team-mate, Pierre van Hooijdonk, who used to celebrate goals that way. As he walked back to collect his jacket, Van der Sar gave Overmars a playful kick on the backside, having previously asked him not to celebrate like that, but who was going to stop him? He had been here since the Velvet Revolution – this was his moment.

'The shirt is still in my bag and will not go to the dry cleaner. It will be framed,' Overmars later said. 'As a player, I never celebrated goals and victories so exuberantly. I actually wanted to do this after Real Madrid, but then I held back. When we won in Turin, I thought I'll just do it. Pierre van Hooijdonk used to do it every week, so I'm allowed to do it once.'

v: A UNIQUE ROMANTICISM

He didn't know it at the time, but Donny van de Beek's equaliser in Turin was scored in the 34th minute, a symbolic time in a symbolic season for Ajax. The number 34 was worn by Abdelhak Nouri, Van de Beek's childhood friend and former team-mate who would've had a key role in this Champions League run. He chose the number 34 when he broke into the first team as Ajax were chasing their 34th league title, but his collapse meant that Ajax would go on this journey without him. For Van de Beek, after a difficult start to the season, this was an emotional moment. Along with Matthijs de Ligt and Frenkie De Jong, he was seen as one of the emerging young stars, and his Champions League performances only enhanced his status.

Born to an Ajax-supporting father, André, the club had been embedded into Donny from a young age. He joined Ajax's youth ranks in 2014 and progressed from there, winning their Talent of the Future award in 2015, as well as making his senior debut under Frank de Boer. His role increased under Peter Bosz but when Erik ten Hag arrived there were doubts whether he would have a long career at Ajax. At the start of the 2018/19 season, he was still seen as a second-choice player, mainly being on the bench and rarely starting games. There were often rumours that season that Van de Beek was leaking stories to *De Telegraaf* – mainly those criticising Ten Hag – but by the second half of the season, the youngster would get his chance.

Like him, Brazilian team-mate David Neres was in the same boat. He signed from São Paulo in January 2017, but action was limited under Ten Hag, so much so that he had an offer for a move to China's Guangzhou Evergrande for a fee exceeding €40m in January 2019. Ajax refused, believing he had a role to play, and here they were after beating Juventus, one of two clubs in Europe, along with Barcelona, with a chance of winning the treble of the league, cup and Champions League. Both Van de Beek and Neres, who had grown in the squad over time, were influential in Juventus's downfall in the quarter-final. Now, it was the defining phase of the season, starting with a match against Groningen.

Groningen and Euroborg is a tough place to visit and this was the most complex challenge in Ajax's four remaining fixtures. Win here, and they basically had a hand on the title. After the youngsters took charge in Turin four days prior, here it needed the experience of Klaas-Jan Huntelaar to seal the win. The forward, 35, had sporadically been used in the Champions League from the group stage onwards, with the 'Tadić variant' sweeping across Europe. Whenever Ten Hag called upon Huntelaar in the league, he delivered. Huntelaar struck in Groningen, then was sent off five minutes later, but Ajax held on and were top of the league. Games came thick and fast at this stage of the season. Just three days after that, Vitesse were swept aside 4-2 and a first title since 2014 was close.

Champions League fever was still across Amsterdam. If Real Madrid and Juventus could be beaten with such ease, surely their next opponents, Tottenham, could be taken apart as well? Tottenham were a club on the rise. Under Mauricio Pochettino, they challenged for the Premier League title in successive seasons, playing brilliant football with players like Harry Kane, Son Heung-min and ex-*Ajacieds* Jan Vertonghen, Toby Alderweireld and Christian Eriksen. They weren't expected to reach the semi-finals of the Champions League – in the previous round, they needed a bit of luck and help from VAR to beat the all-conquering Manchester City of Pep Guardiola.

It was 30 April 2019 – 23 years and two weeks since Ajax last took the field in a Champions League semi-final against Panathinaikos, they were back. It was a different atmosphere, different footballing context, different world, but the Ajax essence was the same. At the Tottenham Hotspur Stadium in north London, which had opened earlier that month, Ajax were ready for Spurs. Once again, Ajax opted for the tried-and-successful Tadić variant and from the off the Dutch side were better. Fifteen minutes in, their dominance paid off. Ziyech received the ball and finely threaded a pass to Van de Beek. Similar to his goal against Juventus where he received the ball from the Moroccan and slotted home, he did the same here, firing past Hugo Lloris as the noise from the 3,000 travelling Ajax fans hit its maximum. In the same half, Van de Beek had another chance but was stopped by the French goalkeeper, while in the second, Neres had a chance to make it two, but his shot agonisingly hit the post.

In the end, it was a 1-0 win and the season was heading in the right direction. Ajax were top of the *Eredivisie*, one hand on the title, they had the lead in the Champions League semi-final on aggregate and in the weekend after beating Tottenham they were to play the KNVB Cup Final against Willem II. Winning the cup isn't usually a big priority for Ajax, but in this extraordinary season, there was great interest. Factor in that they were aiming to win the cup for the first time since 2010 and fans flocked. Ajax were allocated 11,000 tickets for the Rotterdam final, 15,000 travelled and all tickets sold out. At De Kuip, the forward triumvirate of Ziyech, Huntelaar and Tadić were deployed, and they made light work of it. Towards the end of the first half, Blind and Huntelaar scored twice in quick succession, and in the second, the veteran forward added a third before Rasmus Kristensen got the fourth.

At the final whistle, the team were overjoyed. They had a crucial second leg in midweek, but the happiness was palpable – the squad knew they'd be broken apart in a few months, so they wanted to enjoy the moment. When Ajax last won this trophy, Tadić was at a different Dutch club, Huntelaar was in Germany, De Ligt, De Jong, Van de Beek and Neres were still in school, Ziyech was just starting off. This may not have been the ultimate prize, but it was a valuable one in a season that defied expectations. The treble was the dream and one part of it was secured.

Back in Amsterdam, all eyes were on the semi-final again. Neres was injured, so there was the usual nervousness. Before the game, Ten Hag asked for the home support to rise again: 'We start again at 0-0. We are not playing for a draw. We have to win. The ambiance in the Arena has been great all season – that will help us.' Ajax's media team made a video for the match, as they had done all season. They reminded everyone that the job was only half done. On the pitch, Kasper Dolberg returned to the team in place of the injured Neres, while the rest remained the same.

The first half couldn't have gone any better. Five minutes into it, De Ligt, whose mythical rise in Turin propelled Ajax to this point, scored again from a corner, outjumping Dele Alli and finding the back of the net. The Arena erupted, and just 30 minutes later, it happened again. Tadić and Ziyech, involved in so many moments over the course of the season, combined again. The Serb, down the left, found an inward-running Ziyech and he slammed the ball past

Lloris, leaving the Frenchman no chance. It was perfect. Ajax were 2-0 up on the night, 3-0 on aggregate. Nothing could go wrong, surely?

It did. In the second half, Lucas Moura scored. And then he scored again. And then he scored for a third time, right at the death. At full time, a collective groan from the stadium, apart from the small group of travelling Tottenham fans, could be heard. One of the most historic seasons in Ajax's recent years had a bitter ending. Ajax, the darlings of Europe that year, went out in the most heartbreaking way possible. Moura, who was in for the injured Kane, had the match of his life. The post-mortem started soon after: why were De Ligt and Blind going for an attacking free kick at 3-0 up, leaving them exposed to concede Moura's first? Why were André Onana and Lasse Schöne so hesitant in clearing the ball which led to Moura's second? Most painfully: why weren't Ajax able to hold on for a few more seconds?

It was the final few seconds. Spurs had a corner, Lloris came up and nothing came of it – that usually signals the end and the stadium and city breathed a united sigh of relief, but out of nowhere, Moura struck his third. Ajax were out. Tottenham were going to the Champions League Final in Madrid. After the goal and once again after the final whistle, the players fell to the ground, unwilling to look, unwilling to accept and unwilling to understand. Ten Hag, usually so headstrong and composed, was crestfallen on the touchline. The players who spoke to the media could hardly find the right words – who could blame them? This felt cruel.

On Dutch TV, the commentary put it best: 'Football hell: it exits, and Ajax is in it. Unbelievable. Nothing short of a nightmare!' Players were in tears. These young warriors who had grown up loving a broken Ajax took a determined Ajax one step away from a historic final. This team had gripped the country – a record 5.4 million people tuned in, but many didn't get the joy they wanted. In the dressing room, Daley Blind, along with Ten Hag, tried to calm matters, praising the team and reminding them that the season was still on. Speaking to the media, the coach assured his side were ready for the title: 'This group is so resilient, it will be there again on Sunday [in the league].'

In the days that followed, attention turned towards securing the league title. Doubts arose over whether they could do it. The mental strain from the Tottenham defeat may have been too much, but they were eager to prove them wrong. On 12 May, Ajax beat Utrecht: Huntelaar, Van de Beek and Tadić (twice) found the net in a 4-1 win, while PSV fell to AZ. Unofficially, the title was secured – they just needed to win on the final day.

The final game was against De Graafschap at Vijverberg, where Ajax suffered their last great misery on the final day of the 2015/16 season when they lost the title to PSV. It was unlikely something similar could happen here again and Ajax ensured it didn't. It ended 4-1. This was a different team – newer, fresher, hungrier, eager to prove themselves. Ajax were champions again for the first time in six years and they completed the double. In celebrations, the win was dedicated to Nouri. The number 34 was prevalent all around. This was for him.

And so there they were. Huntelaar, the seasoned expert, played his part. De Ligt, the young leader, showed up when needed most and got a deserved transfer to Italian champions Juventus. De Jong, already on his way out, was serene; Tadić, so loved so early in his time, formed a brilliant partnership with Ziyech and provided memories of a lifetime; Van de Beek and Neres were patient and got their reward. There were others too: Onana rose to stardom over the course of the season, Blind's leadership was essential while Schöne, who eventually left for Genoa, had his stunning free kick against Real Madrid go down in history. At a time where football was so heavily dominated by the elite, Ajax had to build from within to compete, and they did so successfully.

For Ten Hag as well, this was important – it wasn't that long ago that he was criticised for decisions, but his impact was massive and evident. By the end of the year, Tadić finished 20th in the running for the Ballon d'Or, while the achievements of the team led to a boom in baby names resembling Ajax stars: compared with 2018, nearly 35 per cent more children were named Donny, 50 per cent more were named Frenkie and 60 per cent more were called Nouri. Financially, the Champions League run brought Ajax €91m – their most prosperous European campaign ever.

While some argue this felt like a season where Ajax detached from the past that somewhat held them back, Peter Drury, who commentated on Ajax matches against Real Madrid, Juventus and Tottenham, tells me he believed this team connected with that of the previous eras: 'There was a romance, regardless of the Ajax teams I had seen in the 1990s or the new century. What it did for me was that it evoked a feeling that I was watching one of the great clubs from its golden era. It connected Ajax to its famous 1970s Cruyff past. It gave them that charisma and magnetism. Those who feel the history of the game, those who feel romantically connected to the game, would naturally attach to Ajax. So, it was like a return of history.'

There was indeed a unique romanticism attached to this team. The intellect of old combined with the innovativeness of the modern era. The most beautiful season in Ajax's recent history concluded with the domestic double and an unlikely but eventually soul-crushing appearance in the Champions League semi-final. This was special. So very special.

PART 3:

AJAX, REINVENTED

REVOLUTION 2.0

*From a frugal policy to one of the
healthiest clubs in Europe*

DURING AJAX'S shareholders' meeting in 2018, chief executive Edwin van der Sar highlighted three aims for the club over the next few years. The first objective was to ensure Ajax would be the undisputed number one in the Netherlands, not just by winning the domestic title, but also by maintaining a strong financial position. The second objective was to ensure that Ajax could mix with Europe's best by promoting players from within and shrewdly using the transfer market. The third objective was to establish that Ajax had the best youth education in football at De Toekomst, furthering the greatness of their academy and giving more talents the chance to make their mark in the first team. Two years prior to that, Van der Sar and director of player policy, Marc Overmars, were under fire for Ajax's downward spiral. By the end of the 2018/19 season, they were praised all over for managing Ajax so smartly and spurring the team on to the semi-finals of the Champions League as well as winning the domestic double. What happened in between?

Ajax's improvement required tweaks and going away from the system that many felt they were heading towards. The 2018/19 campaign raised nostalgia of the great Ajax sides of old, those inspired and heavily influenced by players from their academy and the football was along similar lines. But, the class of 2019, led by Overmars, Van der Sar, finance director Jeroen Slop and chief commercial officer Menno Geelen, had a modern touch. Johan Cruyff famously once said that he's never seen a bag of money score a goal and while that is true, it's also true that bags of money can pay better players to score key goals. Dušan Tadić was one of the faces of that Champions League run, and he was one of the faces of the new Ajax – one that announced that this was a rebirth for the club in a different era, rather than one that reminded people of the old.

It was only in 2010 that a shock had hit Ajax – they had recorded a net loss of €21m, which was the largest ever recorded by a Dutch club and raised concerns over their future. However, under Rik van den Boog, the club recovered quickly and was able to make up the loss. Eventually, the on-pitch success of Frank de Boer's reign ensured that the *Eredivisie* title returned to Amsterdam and that subsequently meant more Champions League football, which, as known, is lucrative to Dutch clubs. The summer of 2011 was the last time Ajax would spend big as the squad was strengthened with a view that the players brought in would help the club for years to come. A total of €13.2m was shed on players including Jasper Cillessen and Kolbeinn Sigthórsson and then, after Overmars's arrival in 2012, the switch was flicked. The former winger made it clear that Ajax would spend frugally to save up more, often causing frustration.

Over the next few years, key players were sold each season and between 2012 and 2015 Ajax had a net spend of €56.7m, having spent €36.6m on incoming transfers and raising €93.35m. No players were purchased for more than €10m, with Daley Sinkgraven's €7m arrival from Heerenveen in 2014 being the most expensive. Factor in the frequent Champions League income and Ajax were building a healthy money pot to dig into. While De Boer's reign, especially the end, isn't widely memorable for the football on the pitch, his success, combined with Overmars's reluctance to spend big, laid the foundations for the future of the club.

REVOLUTION 2.0

By 2018, Ajax had become the healthiest club in Europe with a reserve of over €200m. Entering the summer transfer window of 2018, Ajax had the biggest budget of all teams in the *Eredivisie*, standing at an estimated €90m, well clear of PSV Eindhoven behind them (€73m), as well as a profitable business model. In five of the previous six fiscal years (considering the time period from when Overmars joined), the club had reported a loss just once – €1m in 2016 – while the average profit between 2012 and 2017 was €25m, the highest of which was €67m in 2017. Additionally, between 2012 and 2017, Ajax had made €179m in profit from player sales. The highest amount was raised in 2017 (€79m) when the likes of Davinson Sánchez and Davy Klaassen were sold to Premier League clubs.

It wasn't until 2016 and the late arrival of Hakim Ziyech that the transfer policy was altered and by 2018 and the arrival of Tadić from Southampton and Daley Blind from Manchester United that the wage cap was broken too. The wage cap was set by Cruyff and Theo van Duivenbode in the midst of the Velvet Revolution – a player could earn no more than €1m per year. In time, Overmars and Ajax recognised that this was not going to take them far. The club had the reserves to pay big and they needed to pay big to compete. Potential future players could earn more elsewhere, and it gave current players the invitation to leave. In Simon Kuper and Stefan Szymanski's book, *Soccernomics*, it's backed up that teams with a higher salary budget usually perform better and Ajax now had the money to pay their best players more. And so, they took the chance. Ajax wanted to go far in Europe, and they were open to change.

With Tadić's arrival on a reported €3.5m-a-season salary, a snowball effect was formed which changed the finances and budgeting of the club. The first instance was to make purchases of top players, such as the Serb and Blind in 2018. That led to more rewards for high-performing players, as evident by Hakim Ziyech's raise and contract extension after the transfer window shut that year. Then, existing players were given greater importance too: youngsters like David Neres and Kasper Dolberg were given improved deals and, finally, those in the academy who were expected to have big careers in the future, like Ryan Gravenberch, were also handed a bigger contract as a way to keep them at the club. This was something Ajax, Overmars and Slop were willing to do. The fall of the wage ceiling led to a drastic rise in the amount spent on wages. According to accounts from 2018, Ajax spent €53m on player wages, and that rose to €92m a year later (a rise of 73.5 per cent).

Slop, the former economics graduate who started his career as an accountant at Ernst & Young, had a vital role in this. The longest-serving member of the club management in 2018, having joined immediately after the IPO two decades prior and seen drastic changes including the reign of Uri Coronel, Cruyff's revolution and Overmars's leadership, he had a huge hand in taking the club into this new era. 'We went fishing with a rowboat; we don't have an ocean liner like English clubs,' Slop said to NRC in December 2018. 'Then when you do catch fish in the Premier League, you don't do it with dastardly bait. There is spirited investment there. You have to know where you come from, how you spend your money. Letting go of the salary cap to catch up in Europe? Yes. But to increase the whole cost level ruthlessly is nonsense. We cannot match what is being paid in the Premier League. At the same time we are busy getting those players. They don't come for nothing. Big steps have been made.'

Van der Sar, speaking to *Voetbal International* in 2019, recognised the lack of creative thinking in the transfer market and explained the thought process behind the changes: 'If you saw our budget, it seemed as if everything that Ajax stands for on the field – creative, dominant and offensive – did not apply to the policy in the financial field. We played more passes wide than forward. As directors we said: look at what we have. Ajax has a great name, a top training program, good players are coming [through] and money in the bank. We asked: "Why do we have to act so defensively?" With a Europa League budget you will never perform at Champions League level. The amounts we started paying, including salaries, were actually un-Ajax. We stuck our necks out, because we still had to perform and make it to the Champions League. But we were convinced that it had to be this way. We cannot realise our goal, the step to the top of Europe, with only our own talents.'

Ziyech's signing was the first seed of this changing transfer policy. The Moroccan arrived at the club after a difficult start to the 2016/17 season, and Overmars admitted that he was late to act. From the next summer onwards, Ajax and Overmars identified targets and made their moves sooner to give players more time to adapt to life in Amsterdam. Core targets arrived at the club early in 2017 for manager Marcel Keizer with only Maximilian Wöber's transfer dragging out, being completed at the end of August that year. The same happened in the winter as Nicolás Tagliafico arrived from Independiente within days of the January transfer window opening and Rasmus Kristensen joined too – both were seen as long-term purchases, with the Argentine full-back playing a key role in the club's Champions League run.

It was later that year that the purchases of Tadić and Blind were also done and, more importantly, Ajax formulated a plan to keep hold of their finest young stars. Players like Matthijs de Ligt, André Onana, Kasper Dolberg, Justin Kluivert and Frenkie De Jong were widely touted by Europe's top clubs, but Ajax had a different plan. Van der Sar and Overmars summoned these players to De Toekomst with a video highlighting how essential these players would be for the future of the club. Each player was likened to an Ajax hero of the past with the player relating to the legend through position, nationality or relationship. Onana was compared to Van der Sar. Kluivert was equated to his father, Patrick. De Jong was Christian Eriksen. De Ligt was 1970s icon Barry Hulshoff, and Dolberg was fellow Nordic forward Zlatan Ibrahimović.

Ajax believed this group would be paramount in the coming years and they wanted to show that, like the players of the past, they too could achieve great things with the club. Ultimately, only Kluivert departed that summer, going to Roma, while the rest stayed on. Ajax had completed their transfer business by July that year, in time for the preliminary rounds of the Champions League, and the rest was history. The ones that stayed had a crucial role to play, and in time, many of them were gone too.

POST-MAY 2019

Reaching the semi-finals earned Ajax a grand €78.5m (excluding the €12m earned from ticket receipts), and it was added to by player sales that year. That summer, De Jong was off to Barcelona for an €86m fee (add-ons included), while a deal was agreed for De Ligt with Juventus for €85.5m and Kasper Dolberg was off to Nice for €20.5m, amongst others. At the end of that season, Slop was gone too, and he was replaced by Susan Lenderink, the former accountancy graduate from the University of Amsterdam who held previous roles at PricewaterhouseCoopers and De Bijenkorf, a chain of high-end department stores, where she became chief financial officer in 2012.

By the end of that financial year, Ajax posted record-high revenues, amounting to €199m, which was €106m more than the previous year and driven heavily by their earnings from UEFA. Compared with other clubs, that record earning put them in 23rd in the Deloitte Money League, ahead of the likes of Benfica, Wolverhampton Wanderers and Valencia, but the disparity between the Netherlands and Europe's top football nations put them well behind the others. Barcelona, the leaders of the Money League, had a total revenue of €841m – over four times as much.

A driving force behind those record revenue numbers was the commercial revenue of €60m, the highest in the *Eredivisie*, ahead of Feyenoord, who earned €45m. This was due to the strategy led by chief commercial officer Geelen. A former journalist, Geelen dropped the pen for a role in marketing. He joined Ajax in 2010 and was promoted to head of sponsorships within four months of arriving at the club. Just over two years later, Geelen earned another promotion, this time to commercial director, where he was heavily involved in new sponsorship deals for the club, working closely with Van der Sar to raise the club's commercial potential. Given Dutch clubs don't earn as much through television, sponsorships are vital, and Geelen did a fine job in his time. By 2018, he was the club's chief commercial officer, and his work was widely praised around Europe.

Some of the key deals secured by Geelen included that of shirt sponsor Ziggo, as mentioned earlier, which was extended in 2021 on a €9m-a-year deal until June 2025, as well as that of kit supplier Adidas, on an €8m-a-year deal until June 2025. In addition to that, he formed key international links, more of which will be expanded on later in this book. Geelen recognises that raising sponsorship revenue is of paramount importance. Commercial revenue is often not imperative to clubs in Europe's top leagues, but for Ajax and other Dutch clubs, it is important for survival.

Speaking on the *Ajax Podcast*, he highlighted that ticket prices can't be raised as fans are the lifeblood of the club, and revenues have to be earned through means that don't affect fans: 'If we were to double the prices of our season passes, we would still have no trouble selling out at all. But Ajax is Ajax and has to remain accessible to everyone. Of course, ticket prices fluctuate and are bound to go up every now and then, but we will always keep the increase to a reasonable maximum. We're not looking to grow our income through ticket prices.'

Indeed, selling tickets at the Johan Cruyff Arena is quite an easy task, provided prices are reasonable, which they mostly have been. Ajax's season ticket prices, on average, are the third highest in the Netherlands, behind PSV and Feyenoord. From their 2019 accounts, Ajax earned €51m in matchday revenue, up €19m from their previous year, having been helped by their Champions League run as well as extra matches in the KNVB Cup. This was significantly more than nearest *Eredivisie* rivals Feyenoord, who earned exactly three times less that season (€17m). Ajax's average matchday attendance went over 52,200 that season, some 1,000 more than the previous campaign. This helped make up for the relatively small television prize money Dutch clubs make. In 2018/19, Ajax earned €9.5m in TV money from the *Eredivisie*, where distribution is dependent on the club's results over the previous ten seasons. Ajax are the most successful in that regard, resulting in them earning the most.

The efforts of Geelen and the commercial group at Ajax are immense, but, as highlighted, the record results are considerably lower compared with other European clubs and leagues. While Ajax posted record commercial revenues in 2019, more than the likes of Lyon, Roma, Everton and West Ham, the higher powers of European football earned in excess of €300m in commercial revenues. The likes of Barcelona (€384m), Paris Saint-Germain (€363m), Bayern Munich (€357m), Real Madrid (€355m) and Manchester United (€317m) all had a clear gap. Still, it's a crucial aspect of Ajax's recent financial resurgence.

As their stars of 2019 left, replacements were brought in from abroad: Razvan Marin (€12.5m) joined from Standard

Liège to bolster the midfield, Lisandro Martínez (€7m) came in from Defensa y Justicia and Edson Álvarez (€15m) joined from Club América – they were there to shore up the backline, while more experienced additions were made in the form of Quincy Promes (€15.7m) and Ryan Babel (loan). Overall, this was Ajax's most expensive summer outlay ever. Nearly €60m was spent in total. As is often the case, losing key players and bringing in plenty doesn't always go as planned and while they were at the top in the Netherlands, challenging for the title, their European campaign didn't pan out well. Ajax were paired with Chelsea, Valencia and Lille and finished third, dropping down to the Europa League, where they lost to Getafe in an ill-tempered round of 32 clash. In March 2020, the domestic season was suspended and subsequently called off as the COVID-19 pandemic affected football around Europe.

The *Eredivisie* was one of a few European leagues to end their season prematurely. Ajax were top of the league, and, unlike the French Ligue 1 which was also cancelled, the *Eredivisie* didn't award the title to anyone. Instead, they allowed clubs to qualify for European competition based on their final league position when the season was brought to an abrupt end. Ajax reached the Champions League for the 2020/21 season but the pandemic did affect their finances. The club reported revenues of €162m for 2019/20, €37m less than the previous year, although they were still their second-highest revenue figures ever. This was largely due to their lack of European progress and a fall in matchday revenues.

Despite the fall, from a domestic perspective Ajax were still healthier than other clubs. Ajax's revenue was more than that of Feyenoord and PSV Eindhoven combined and supported theories that the Amsterdam side could become the Bayern Munich of the Netherlands. However, given the differences between the Dutch and German football markets in terms of television proceeds, merchandising and sponsorship, it seems unlikely Ajax will become like Bayern: the record Dutch champions are reliant on matchday income for their revenues, and that isn't the case for clubs in Europe's top leagues. One season out of the Champions League competition proper could be detrimental. Additionally, clubs like Bayern can hold on to their players for a long time, which isn't the case for Ajax, as Overmars once said: 'They [Bayern Munich] can easily bind their players for four or five years. Here, they are itching to leave after two, three years. The club is constantly having to deal with the fact it is having its players taken away from it. On that basis, you can't win forever.'

In the summer of 2020, more players from the Champions League side of 2019 departed. Donny van de Beek went to Manchester United for €39m, while Hakim Ziyech went to Chelsea for €40m, making that Ajax side the most expensive in *Eredivisie* history as players from that squad brought the club over €285m (including bonuses). This was now, effectively, a new cycle for Ajax, but with it came some old flavour. Former players Davy Klaassen and Maarten Stekelenberg returned, while transfers from abroad were still made with a view to the long run. Antony was signed from São Paulo and Mohammed Kudus came in from Nordsjælland. In addition to that, the pathway from the academy was still open as Jurriën Timber and Ryan Gravenberch were to be given more opportunities in the first team.

The season ended with a double of the league and cup, meaning that in coach Ten Hag's two full seasons at the club, he was able to win both domestic titles twice. It was also their most impressive league campaign in years as Ajax finished 16 points clear of second-placed PSV, scoring 102 goals and conceding just 23. In Europe, another complicated Champions League group of Liverpool, Atalanta and Midtjylland resulted in a third-place finish and subsequent Europa League entry – a run which ended at the quarter-final stage when they lost to Roma. This was also the season where Ajax broke their transfer record with the signing of Sébastien Haller from West Ham United for a €22.5m fee in January 2021, reuniting with Ten Hag after their Utrecht days. He also earned the highest annual salary of any Ajax player at a reported €5m a season (excluding bonuses) – more than that of Tadić. Unfortunately, due to an administrative error, he was not registered for their Europa League squad.

From their accounts for 2020/21, which covered the year that COVID-19 most affected football, there were some important conclusions and effects on the club:

- The club made a €12m loss, or €8m after taxes (which was still significantly lower than other top European clubs). This was only the second time since 2010 that Ajax recorded an annual loss.
- Net revenue amounted to €125.2m, a decrease of €37.1m due to lower matchday revenues, mainly due to playing without fans in stadiums.
- The revenue figures were still the third highest they had ever recorded.
- The sale of players like Van de Beek and Ziyech was beneficial to their income.
- Ajax's commercial revenue rose to €68m (up five per cent).
- Ajax were still heavily reliant on income from player sales and qualification for the Champions League.

GLOBAL SCOUTING

Ajax's global scouting network has improved drastically since 2018, with Overmars making it clear that he wanted to have the best scouts he could find working with the club. Their success in reaching the 2017 Europa League Final with a squad that had a fine mix of talent developed at the club (such as De Ligt, Onana and Klaassen) and players brought in from abroad or other clubs (such as Sánchez, Ziyech and Neres) created an ambition to close the gap between youth scouting and professional scouting (i.e. scouting for the first team) and Ajax made appointments to help them reach that goal. In 2018, Michel Doesburg joined the club as the youth scouting coordinator. Having had a playing career spanning nearly two decades, he worked for AZ Alkmaar as a youth coach and scout before moving to Amsterdam in the summer of 2018.

Supporting him was the head of youth recruitment, Casimir Westerveld, who had been at the club since 2006, working in various roles with the youth squads before being promoted to his position in 2018. In his role, he is in charge of bringing in the finest young talents to train at the club and he has a team of permanent Ajax employees and hundreds of volunteers around the Netherlands who monitor talented players. According to him, a typical Ajax player in any age group has to show four basic principles in his profile as a footballer: technical actions, tactical principles, motor performance and mental skills, and these form the modern Ajax player.

From a broader perspective, there are more people around the world who hunt for foreign talent with a view to joining Ajax. In 2018, Belgian Urbain Haesaert returned to the club as a scout in Belgium and France. He previously worked for Ajax between 2004 and 2010 before moving to Anderlecht. Haesaert's return was met with great excitement: in his previous stint, the likes of Jan Vertonghen, Toby Alderweireld and Thomas Vermaelen were all brought to Amsterdam. At youth level, Angelo De Gruyter was signed in 2019 having also previously worked at Anderlecht. His portfolio of talents he found included Romelu Lukaku, Dennis Praet and Leander Dendoncker.

John Steen Olsen had been with Ajax since 1995, working through the successful Louis van Gaal era, the shaky 2000s and, eventually, the Ajax of Overmars. He continued to scout the Scandinavian region. The other international scouts involved were Fred Arroyo, who had been with Ajax since 2004, Roy Wesseling, who joined in 2010, Sonny Bosz (the son of former Ajax coach Peter Bosz), who joined in 2020, Hans van der Zee, who had been there since 2007, and Henk Veldmate, who joined from Groningen in 2016 and was mainly involved with the club's scouting of South American talents, more of which is explained later. Together, they formed the international core, travelling and using their links to find players abroad.

Often, they have been criticised for spending too much on players who aren't yet ready for the first team and even for using intermediaries who sometimes work to serve their own interests. Often, they've also been criticised for missing out on key targets, with the most notable examples being right-back Timothy Castagne from Genk and left-back Jérôme Roussillon from Montpellier, but that is normal for a football club. Ajax don't have the same number of scouts as other top European clubs, nor do they have the same budget for it, but it's still a commendable effort over the last few years to bring them to where they are.

Ajax have had to budget differently when signing players in recent times: for players that cost over €6m, the management needs approval from the supervisory board to approve the transfer and for a long period, until the signing of Haller, there was a maximum budget of €20m for a transfer. Between 2016 and 2021, there have been 17 transfers upwards of €6m as the club has been more willing to loosen the purse strings to improve their squad.

With relatively healthy financial performances, even during a pandemic when their matchday revenue was impacted, the club have been able to invest, and while there is the occasional transfer which doesn't work out, it has been a steady ship under the leadership of Overmars. The former winger's work is a collaboration with others at the club: for him and his plans to be successful, he needs great efforts from others, such as Lenderink, Geelen and Van der Sar. They're like a rowing team: all their members need to be at their uniform best to thrive.

A LITTLE SAMBA,
A LITTLE GRINTA

Ajax delve into South America

IN 2019, ahead of their opening Champions League group stage match against Lille, Ajax took out a full-page newspaper advertisement in four countries: the United States of America, Mexico, Argentina and Brazil. In the ads, there was a portrait of players from that nation that played for the club. In Brazil, it was David Neres, in the USA, Sergiño Dest, in Mexico, Edson Álvarez and in Argentina, Nicolás Tagliafico and Lisandro Martínez. Alongside a picture of the players, there was a little message.

The Brazilian version, for example, read (translated from Portuguese):

> Hi Brazil,
> We, Ajax Amsterdam, have something to say to you.
> You will undoubtedly remember last season, when our boys amazed the world by playing with the Ajax philosophy. With players from our own youth academy and international talents.

Today we start a new journey in the
Champions League. We do so with the same
philosophy and dream, to make history.
Come with us.
Step into our dream.
Join David's dream.
Let this journey become an
unforgettable dream.
Thank you and see you soon,
AFC Ajax.

Similar messages were sent in the USA, Mexico and
Argentina in English and Spanish, accompanied with the
headline 'Join the Future'. Ajax won the match against Lille
3-0, with Álvarez finding the net, and it was the perfect day
for Ajax's marketing team, the scouts as well as the team on
the pitch. The advertisement and win were the embodiment
of Ajax's rekindled relationship with the region. Since 2016,
in a process led by Marc Overmars, Ajax have scouted and
recruited extensively from Latin and South America. Ajax
did previously have some history with South America,
having played host to players like Maxwell and Luis Suárez
in the 21st century. However, their record wasn't the best.
Earlier in the century, they signed players such as Darío
Cvitanich, Nicolás Lodeiro, Gastón Sangoy and Filipe Luís
and they didn't live up to expectations, prompting Ajax to
look away from the region.

It was in the summer window of 2016 and the dual
transfers of Colombians Davinson Sánchez and Mateo
Cassierra from Atlético Nacional and Deportivo Cali,
respectively, for a combined fee of €10.5m that Ajax began
to rekindle that interest. At the time, Sánchez had a vital

role to play in Nacional's Copa Libertadores win, while Cassierra was an emerging star. Overmars felt there was great value in South American players. He noted that clubs from Europe's top leagues had greater access to European players or, more specifically, Scandinavian players that Ajax always followed, and that the Amsterdam side had to start looking elsewhere. This was contrary to what Overmars had said previously. In 2013, he ruled out South American signings, citing the complications in third-party ownership, but that soon changed. Fortunately for them, it worked out.

'The mentality of players from South America is often different, complementary to the footballers we have in the Netherlands,' Overmars said to *Algemeen Dagblad* in 2019. 'I've said before that in terms of mentality and attitude you don't just see ten De Ligts coming out of training. So our scouts look for such qualities elsewhere. That way we can strengthen the team. Scouting in Denmark or Belgium, for example, can be very successful. We still do that. But there are five million people living in Denmark. In Brazil, a country that has been world champion five times, there are over 200 million.'

Ajax have enviable riches in the Netherlands, and with that comes an unmatchable pull and attraction for prospective young players. However, for South Americans and, more specifically, Brazilians, Ajax aren't the number one in the country. Instead, it's PSV Eindhoven, whose track record with Brazilians is excellent. PSV developed strong links in the country and formed key scouting networks through their primary sponsors, Philips, and they reaped the rewards from it through the success of players such as Romário and Ronaldo. Both had their first spells in Europe with the Eindhoven club, making PSV the leading club for

South Americans looking to find their way in the continent. It was evident once again on a wider scale in 2005 when PSV reached the semi-finals of the Champions League under the tutelage of Guus Hiddink and had five South American players in the side including Heurelho Gomes, Alex and Jefferson Farfán.

Ajax wanted to change that, and the triumph of Sánchez leveraged them for future players. Factor in the addition of scout Henk Veldmate, who had a good reputation of dealing with South American talent, and there was the recipe for a better relationship with the continent's emerging talents. Veldmate was most popular in the Netherlands for the discovery of Suárez, having made the trip to the Uruguayan capital of Montevideo to get the forward's signature. The scout worked at fellow Dutch club Groningen for 21 years in directorial and scouting positions, before joining Ajax in 2016 at a time when they were still getting to grips with the transfer market under Overmars. It was Overmars who made Veldmate's arrival possible – the two had a fine relationship over the years, which started when the former winger was working at Go Ahead Eagles.

In addition to Suárez, Veldmate was successful at Groningen with the discovery and signings of players like Erik Nevland, Marcus Berg, Tim Matavž, Dušan Tadić and Virgil van Dijk. Although the signings of Sánchez and Neres in January 2017 for a €12m fee were orchestrated by a scout already at Ajax, Hans van der Zee, it was soon after when Veldmate's impact was shown: he had a crucial role in the purchase of Tagliafico from Independiente, also in the winter window of 2017. Furthermore, while some of Veldmate's best signings have been South Americans, he insists that it's not his sole area of expertise; instead, he credits his joint effort with Van der Zee for Ajax's recent South American success.

Van der Zee has been at Ajax longer, having joined from rivals PSV in 2007. He was at the Eindhoven club for 16 years, and introduced many players to European football, such as those mentioned above that reached the semi-finals of the Champions League in 2005. Van der Zee saw changes aplenty at Ajax and even went through Johan Cruyff's revolution unscathed, despite a widespread belief that he would be gone. Together, he and Veldmate have formed solid links in the continent and the club have benefitted.

With a new approach towards South American talent, Ajax have taken steps to make players feel more at home having recognised the difficulties of moving to Europe, especially when they're young adults or teenagers. Eager to eliminate the mistakes of old, which caused several players to feel unsettled in Amsterdam, they have made appointments and changed habits to ensure youngsters can adapt as quickly as possible. In 2006, Herman Pinkster joined the club, and he was in charge of the administrative and social integration of players into the squad, not just from abroad, but locally as well. He helps players like they're newborns, teaching them the way of life, the methods and standards of the club. Within a year of Pinkster joining, he learned Spanish to help new signings Gabri and Roger García, who joined from Barcelona and Villarreal, respectively, in 2006, and those skills have been useful ever since, even for the new Ajax.

Within the club, Pinkster is seen as a key cog in the machine. If players have issues or concerns, they go to him. If players need recommendations for where to eat or unwind, Pinkster is the man. If players need to sort out their new homes or cars, Pinkster has a way. Such is the relationship between Pinkster and his players that they stay in touch even after they leave: Suárez invited him to his wedding while many others often call or visit. He also helps solve the language barrier. At Ajax, with non-English speaking players, there are three lessons a week with the aim of helping players understand English quickly. This wasn't the case before, as Dutch was the primary language, which many players failed to grasp. Additionally, there's also the Ajax handbook of Dutch football concepts, terminology, rules, regulation and a history of Amsterdam to help foreign players understand what they're getting into. While management like this existed before and has existed at several clubs, it's a significantly different way of doing things than ever before for Ajax.

It was in 2017 when Ajax started seeing the success of their South American mission. Sánchez left for Tottenham Hotspur for a grand €42m fee – over eight times what he was signed for – and while the other two Colombians in the side, Cassierra and Luis Manuel Orejuela, weren't able to make quite the same impact, Sánchez's sale made up for it and gave them the freedom to strengthen their transfer budget.

Cassierra, now at Russian club PFC Sochi, tells me about his experiences at Ajax and what it was like to sign for them: 'I knew about the rumour. Logically, it was not only up to me but also up to the club to let me go and in the end it happened. I chose Ajax because it is a big club with a lot of history. It wasn't easy at the beginning as it was my first experience in European football. It was a different culture, a different language, but with the passing of time I was able to adapt and feel better.' On how Ajax helped him adapt to the club and new surroundings, he says: 'I had an English teacher at the club. I started to learn the language and as time went by I understood more and then it was easier to communicate with all the people at the club, my colleagues and coaches.'

Cassierra's time at the club wasn't as fruitful as other South Americans in later years, but it was vital to have others like him at the club at the same time, and the presence of his compatriot Sánchez was beneficial: 'It was very easy to have a Colombian partner with me at the club. We always talked and supported each other, and we did almost everything together.' Although he was at the club for a three-year period and had two loan spells away, the Colombian feels it was an important event in his career: 'I always trained at 100 per cent to play but I had very few opportunities in the first team. Still, it was an unforgettable experience that helped me grow as a player and as a person.'

Ajax then diversified into other South American nations after Colombia: Tagliafico's winter arrival in 2018 gave him time to settle in and, over the next few years, more Argentines were signed. Lisandro Magallán joined in January 2019 from Boca Juniors for €9m with a view that he was Matthijs de Ligt's successor while Lisandro Martínez moved later that summer from Defensa y Justicia for a €7m fee. The two have had contrasting fortunes: Magallán has had loan spells away, struggling to break into the Ajax side, while Martínez's versatility has gone down well with Erik ten Hag. He has performed well in midfield and defence and even earned a call-up to the Argentinian national team, being a part of their Copa América-winning side in 2021.

The flair comes from Brazil, and Ajax have been hugely successful in the signing of Brazilian wingers. Neres was the first and he was crucial for Ajax in their 2019 Champions League run, while also progressing on the international scene, becoming a full international. Given his success, Ajax moved for another gifted winger in the form of Antony in 2020 for a €15.25m fee. Signed on the recommendation of Van der Zee, he too joined from São Paulo and is expected to have a bright future having played and won gold at the Olympics with Brazil in Tokyo. Additionally, Danilo was signed as a youth player from Santos and had positive stints with Jong Ajax as well as on loan with FC Twente, while a similar move was made for Giovanni, the young attacking midfielder. Overall, Ajax's Brazilian quartet have been valuable signings, contributing effectively and providing the club with potential for the long run. North of Brazil, Ajax also looked at Mexico, signing Edson Álvarez from Club América and, like Martínez, his versatility has also been handy.

There are some signings that didn't happen, too. In 2017, Ajax were close to bringing in Richarlison from Fluminense but were trumped by Watford. Given how his career has gone, he would undoubtedly have become a favourite in Amsterdam. Two years later, an 18-year-old Diego Lainez was close to moving from Club América but that fell through too, and he went to Real Betis instead. I asked Edwin van der Sar about this change in approach when he was at the Dubai International Sports Conference in 2019, and he highlighted that the addition of different footballing cultures to the squad was beneficial: 'Four or five years ago, we were focusing a lot on the Scandinavian regions but because they're very much like the Dutch talents we felt we needed to go for something else, which is why we started looking at South America. Players like Neres from Brazil and Tagliafico and Martínez from Argentina and now we're looking at Mexico too. That way, we can find the right balance between South American *grinta* and the Dutch or European style and provide more experience to the players.'

While it has been mostly successful, some aren't a fan of the new method. Marco van Basten was particularly sceptical, highlighting the huge amount of money spent on Antony, saying he'd prefer if they promoted from within: 'At Ajax, they have a very big mouth: [they say] our youth education is so great. But if you hit yourself so terribly in the chest that the youth education is so great, then of course it is ridiculous that you are going to buy a youth player from Brazil for €25m [bonuses included]. The youth academy is the jewel of Ajax. And then you have to spend your money on boys who guide the younger players. Guys of a certain level and a certain age, such as Daley Blind and Dušan Tadić – that is the balance that you have to find between youth and other players.'

Between 2016 and 2021, Ajax signed eight players from South American clubs for a combined fee slightly over €73m and while some of them didn't have the long careers that were expected, most have been worthwhile additions. The ones that do succeed have an immense connection with the community, as evident by the 2019 hit 'Herres' by rapper Sevn Alias and produced in collaboration with the club. This was the unofficial anthem of Ajax's Champions League season sung by the Amsterdam-raised artist and he had lines for most players of that team.

The catchiest lines, and those along the chorus, were reserved for the team's two South American stars, Tagliafico and Neres: *'Ik heb je back net Nico, Nico Tagliafico'* (I got your back like Nico, Nico Tagliafico) and *'Ik zet herres, ik zet herres, Opdie flank als David Neres'* (I create chaos, I create chaos – on the flank like David Neres). The song was frequently played amongst fans and a video of the players singing it in the changing rooms, led by Neres, went viral. On YouTube, the song has over 5.6 million views (as of November 2021). It was the perfect encapsulation of the South American players at the club: they were loved like they were Amsterdam's own.

Ajax are constantly on the lookout for top talents around the world and the new Ajax finds in South America have been one of their success stories. As is normal in football, every transfer isn't a triumphant one, but the good outweighs the bad for them. For every Magallán and Orejuela there's a Neres and Tagliafico, and while there isn't a guarantee these players will stay at the club for long, when they're doing well there's a bond between themselves and the fans. After they go, there's financial gain for the club that helps fund their next big star. It's a smart strategy constructed after trial and error, shrewd appointments and having the right minds in one place.

DE TOEKOMST,
WITH RONALD DE BOER

De Toekomst, Ajax's world-famous academy

INCLUDING AJAX players, at any given time, it is estimated that up to 35 footballers playing in the *Eredivisie* have received an education at Ajax's academy. It's a testament to their excellence and academy model that so many are able to have top-flight careers once they go through the club's academy. Their hall of fame is a who's who of Dutch footballing icons: from Johan Cruyff, its greatest product, to Johan Neeskens, Marco van Basten to Edwin van der Sar, Dennis Bergkamp to Wesley Sneijder, Edgar Davids to Clarence Seedorf and more. League winners, European Cup winners, treble winners and Ballon d'Or winners have come through the famous walls, been through the Ajax way and emerged as world stars, and as one goes through and succeeds, another is always in the making. At Ajax, the process never stops.

The philosophy at the academy was inspired by the methods of Ajax greats including Jack Reynolds, Vic Buckingham, Rinus Michels and Cruyff: a clear plan that revolved around teamwork, togetherness, attacking football, keeping fans entertained and working around the famed Ajax 4-3-3, which captured the attention of the football world over the course of decades. For many Dutch youngsters, this is the pinnacle, and abroad many aspire to reach Ajax's heights. It's fair to say that without Ajax there would be no *La Masia* in Barcelona, which is why the two clubs share such a close bond. For decades, the youth at Ajax trained at Voorland, but after their decision to move stadiums, the decision was also made to improve their training and youth facilities, citing the need for modernisation.

Plans were first put in place in 1990 and by 1995 renovation and work on Sportpark de Toekomst commenced. A year later, it was complete, and De Toekomst, which translates to 'The Future', was born. Located some 600 metres from the new Amsterdam Arena, this factory of football talent was to embody everything Ajax were all about and they knew that, although winning was an important factor for the club, progression, growth and, most notably, enjoyment of the game, were just as crucial. At a time when Ajax were caught up in a situation where their foreign rivals made more money than them through either their respective leagues paying well or investment into clubs, they had to rely on their own, and for that reason the footballing education at the club is top-notch.

I had the pleasure of speaking to Ronald de Boer to understand his role and more on the modern facility that continuously produces world-beating talent. Well known for his playing days with Ajax and the Dutch national team, De Boer is now an ambassador of Ajax and is frequently involved with De Toekomst with a view towards promoting it to the world. He's been through the system, and now he wants to encourage the next generation to follow his footsteps. 'I'm an ambassador of Ajax, like many ex-players do for other clubs,' he tells me. 'We have ambassadors abroad in places like Japan, China and America and I'm involved in that. Having been brought up by the youth system, I have the knowledge of it and the philosophy we use. Additionally, two times a week I'm on the pitch with the U17s and U18s and there I work closely with four top Ajax youth players who I mentor, so we go into depth using video analysis, what they have to do and what they can do. We try to see where we can get better and we form a future plan.'

For years, De Toekomst was the home for Ajax's youth and reserve teams as well as Jong Ajax, but from 2009 onwards, it also housed the senior team and eventually, Ajax Vrouwen – the women's side – when they were founded in 2012. There, all teams have different staff but a similar outlook towards football with the belief being that a single philosophy is pivotal to making the jump from junior to senior football easier. The *totaalvoetbal* approach and emphasis on the 4-3-3 is vital and what has enabled stars make a near seamless transition to the first team. Change is constant in terms of coaching and staff, with more people employed to improve performances and individual players, but the idea is still the same.

The facility consists of five grass football pitches, two artificial-turf pitches and a grandstand of 2,250 seats, which was named after Bobby Haarms in 2009 following his death that year. Haarms was a former Ajax player in the 1950s, but his most prominent work came as an assistant manager and scout during their golden period from the 1970s all the way to the Louis van Gaal era and beyond. He had a huge hand in the success of their academy. Along with that comes offices, administration rooms, a canteen and a sports hall.

This is the facility where 220 aspiring footballers along with staff spend much of their time.

De Boer highlights the key principles that make De Toekomst so successful: 'When I was there, it was totally different compared with the boys arriving now. We have so many people working in different areas of football both physically and mentally and the education. There are the physical coaches who make sure the boys are fit and the skills coaches, like me, who talk to the boys who play in similar positions to us. I give my guidance about how they can position themselves in the game or how to attack the ball and where they can improve in that position. What we do now at Ajax is so much bigger than when I was younger because back then it was only the head coach and nothing else but now it's five to six people on the pitch overlooking 22 boys, so it's a totally different situation but it's very good, of course. I think it's all for the development of the individuals. They have to learn how to play as a team and, for us, we want to improve the individual. Our aim is to deliver potential Champions League-level players to the first team.'

Ajax wish to intensify the revered Dutch creative thinking in football and that begins with how they scout for players. The *Talentdagen* – talent day – where hopeful footballers take the first steps towards a potential Ajax career, is a popular event. Players have to show that they can control and distribute the ball as well as display their footballing intelligence. That is the first stamp on the passport. Away from that, the scouting network is constantly on the hunt as around 50 scouts scour the Netherlands, going through the streets, local tournaments and football events trying to find the finest talent. Across Europe, the club has also set up key links, as evident from the intake of players like Jan Vertonghen and Christian Eriksen in recent times.

Like with the rest of the club, the Cruyff-inspired Velvet Revolution was a turning point for the academy, with the Dutch great pointing out how the institution was no longer able to produce players who had the ability to play at a Champions League level. The ideas were forgotten and foreign, unassociated methods were adopted. Additionally, there was a clear gap between the first team and academy with the former unable to integrate or associate with the methods of the age groups below them. That needed a swift change. Staff members left, scouts came and went, coaches had to go and the magic of old had to return. De Boer highlights it as a major modern event in De Toekomst's relatively young history.

'I think it was very important – we lost the way of thinking about where Ajax were standing,' the former midfielder says. 'The identity was lost. The focus of how to develop the boys as real Ajax players was gone. That's when Johan Cruyff stepped in at the right moment. For example, Martin Jol was head coach at the time, and he was more of a results-based coach. He only looked to the first team and the needs of the first team.'

That was crucial. At Ajax, it was always clear that the head coach needed to know what was happening with the youths: which player could make the step up, which player was lacking and which player needed more time. The idea was for the academy to promote at least three players to the first team every two years and, if that was not possible, the Ajax carousel would not work.

'A real Ajax coach needs to know what's happening at youth level,' De Boer continues. 'When my brother [Frank de

Boer] was head coach of the first team [after Jol], he always looked at the games of the U13s all the way to the U18s and knew exactly what was happening in the academy. That is so important – that you don't buy a player who you're not 100 per cent sure of, that you don't pay a big fee for a player you may already have in your academy, who has potential and who may possibly even be better. We needed to give our own players a chance rather than spending needlessly. Now, we have coaches who are not afraid to put youngsters into the first team – that's how players like Matthijs de Ligt, Frenkie de Jong and now Ryan Gravenberch, Jurriën Timber and Noussair Mazraoui got a chance.'

So what makes the ideal Ajax coach and footballer in the modern era? The two are quite interlinked. An Ajax player needs to read the game, think ahead, needs to be on top of the game and understand their surroundings. It's not just about winning games, scoring goals or keeping clean sheets – a collective philosophy right from the top to the bottom is essential. Coaches need to be able to adapt to different age groups too. They have to know when a player is ready and realise that by the time a player reaches the age of 17 they have been prepared for the first-team environment. At Ajax, the belief has always been that the whole club is one family and that's what makes De Toekomst so unique.

Ingrained in the academy is the TIPS model – Technique, Insight, Personality and Speed – and within these are ten criteria that the club searches for in their players. All players are given a sheet where their achievements and growth are noted down to identify progress, and while it's impossible for every player to make it to the first team, this education is invaluable, often for other *Eredivisie* clubs. Within De

Tockomst is also the Ajax coaching academy, giving aspiring coaches the chance to hone their skills the Ajax way.

So prestigious is the Ajax way that other clubs want a piece of it too. Barcelona are well-known examples, but clubs across the world are always eager to pick up their methods – in 2020, commercial director Menno Geelen told Sky Sports that others often visited their facilities for tips, but with so many requests, they had to decline plenty. Now, they form partnerships to help others reach their goals and are linked with over 50 clubs in the Netherlands, as well as others in Australia, Japan and China in exchange for a fee.

De Boer on what modern Ajax talent should be like: 'The coach must have the ability to see the potential of players and see the potential of being a typical Ajax player. They must have the principles that we stand for. They must aim forwards and not backwards, be willing to be on the ball. For example, as a defender, you have to know how to move the ball forwards, we must press high up the pitch and the forwards have to be the first line of defence – they must have the individual quality to dribble past defenders and be able to win the ball high up the pitch while linking up well with their team-mates. Those are the things that signify a modern Ajax player and that should be identifiable by a head coach. They must think these boys have the potential to be first-team players because we have so many players who want to become professional footballers, but they can't fit into the system of the club as they sometimes may not be able to conform to the methodologies that we use.'

And who are some of the key figures at De Toekomst at the moment? 'It's difficult to answer because the coach of the U18s is usually the flagship. At Jong Ajax, there is John Heitinga. Of course, the head of the academy, Saïd Ouaali, is vital to maintain the structure. We have so many people working and there are some with a leading role, but we all do it together. The philosophy of Ajax involves winning and this starts from a young age. Everyone wants to win against Ajax, so we have to be prepared and understand how to be on top. The philosophy of Johan Cruyff always exists. We need to have good results with high pressing, maintaining the five-second rule and all those things and those are ingrained in us.'

Saïd Ouaali is one of the chief figures at Ajax and he has a distinct background in the game. Born in Morocco, he moved to the Netherlands at the age of 11 with little knowledge of football, but soon it would become his life. He too had a dream of going professional but could only play at an amateur level as an attacking player, representing the likes of Diemen, Haarlem and, of course, Ajax. But it was his coaching education at famous sports school, CIOS, in Arnhem, that got him a career in football, and he started off with FC Lisse as a coach in 2004 before moving to FC Volendam and, eventually, Ajax in 2012. Ouaali credits his work with disabled children as it aided his development as a coach and he continued to help them part-time when he started at Ajax.

It was Wim Jonk that brought Ouaali to Ajax and he started off as a youth coach in March 2012, working his way up the ladder. In 2014, he led a talented group of U17s featuring Donny van de Beek and Abdelhak Nouri to Future Cup victory before being bumped up to the U19s. His reputation was solid and, during the Technical Heart conflict which led to the departures of Cruyff, Jonk and Ruben Jongkind, Ouaali stayed and was appointed as the interim head of academy, with backing from Edwin van der Sar and Bergkamp. As Ajax searched for a new leader, Ouaali continued to astonish and that prompted the club to keep him as their man. He eventually got the job on a full-time basis.

Now, Ouaali oversees the academy as well as the progress Jong Ajax are making, and De Boer explains the standard practices for a player coming through De Toekomst: 'It's a very intense schedule. They are based at De Toekomst and they go to school in Amsterdam. They train twice a day; sometimes it's football training along with skills training. Sometimes it's football training along with power. Sometimes it's only skills and in school they have to do some voluntary community work. It's all part of their curriculum. It's a very busy schedule. At times I feel it may not be good for the boys because a normal boy, after school, would go out, meet his friends and have a good time but it's different with Ajax boys. They're so occupied with Ajax. On the other hand, however, we see that they need those 10,000 hours. The rule is that if you want to maximise your talent, you need 10,000 hours on the pitch, and the schedule gets you closer to that number. They are repeating and repeating because the more you practise, the better you can get.'

At De Toekomst, football and education go hand in hand. While not all players will make it at Ajax, many may not have football careers at all and it's essential to Ajax that they prepare them for the future elsewhere, which is why the policy has always been that students have to perform well at school in order to get time on the pitch. The quality of education at De Toekomst is also very high and they recognise the relationship between academic and sporting development, encouraging them to take the front foot in a player's academic education. Over the years, they've taken further steps to emphasise the significance of education, as highlighted with the creation and opening of *De School van de Toekomst* – The School of the Future – which opened in September 2015.

Some of the facilities in this school include:

- Fully-equipped kitchen designed to teach youngsters more about nutrition and how to cook.

- Social space with a large video screen for players and staff to meet, present and discuss.

- Open administration area overlooking the reserve team's football pitch where tutors teach.

- Multimedia space where students can learn to sing, dance or perform other recreational activities such as yoga.

- Area for sleeping pods where players are often asked to relax.

- Terrace overlooking the first-team training pitch.

- The Johan Cruyff Arena in clear sight.

De Boer on the importance of the link between academic and footballing education: 'Everybody sees the potential of the boys but when they come into the academy, we have people giving them the education that they would also get at a normal school. They have to work as hard as they can and if you're not doing well at school, you're not allowed to train. Additionally, we have to see the physical condition of the players, like if they have too much fat on their body. We have set standards depending on how old they are because when they're 12 it's obvious that their body mass index will be different to when they're 16 or 17. The players have to focus on all things because only one to five per cent of players will make it into the first team – it's a low percentage. Most of the boys won't make it to the first team so they need to be doing well at school and that is something they have to realise. They need to put in the effort. If they don't do well at school, they need to get better to train with the team and that is something we keep an eye on.'

Ajax wish to educate their players in the best possible way, highlighting the need for their general schooling to be supplemented with financial education for players and their families as well personal development plans, identifying where a player needs to grow. To help with their education, there is also the finest modern technology used at De Toekomst. The most prominent feature is the miCoach Performance Centre, made in collaboration with kit sponsors Adidas and the Vrije University in Amsterdam. This indoor sports hall opened in 2011 and houses a full-size training pitch in a controlled weather environment as well as an advanced 3D science centre used by all teams at the club. At the centre, the club are able to monitor biometric and biomechanical data to understand a player's physical attributes and potential.

Additionally, Ajax also make great use of virtual reality to help players work on their decision-making during games and actions. This is useful to discuss individual actions, unlike trainings which are filmed on video, where you learn more about the team and its structure. With VR, videos of games can be modelled in 3D to allow players to review their own actions. Ajax are constantly in contact with local universities and research centres such as the Netherlands Organisation for Applied Scientific Research to further understand how to improve the use of technology to aid their young players. These relationships are critical in the long run.

Responsible for these technological changes in recent times is Max Reckers, who started his football career with Van Gaal as a video analyst and innovation architect at AZ Alkmaar. With Van Gaal, he also went to Bayern Munich and Manchester United as well as the Dutch national team, and in that period, he also helped set up the miCoach Performance Centre, working closely with Ajax in 2011. Since 2017, he has been with Ajax on a permanent basis as a performance technology consultant and his expertise is valuable to De Toekomst.

De Boer: 'Technology is very useful for us. We don't think the old ways are the way to go forward. We have to adapt to the current situation, and we have the technology and data for that. We monitor everything. One of the key things we now know that helps close the gap between the youth teams and the first team is that we know the physical needs of players. We know the kilometres they run and that younger players were having fewer intense runs.'

He adds: 'For example, for the boys who were 17 years old and joining the first team or Jong Ajax for training two or three times in a week, we learned that on the ball there was no problem at all. But, without the ball, when they were running, they would struggle after a few weeks of training and they got injured or they would slow down because they couldn't keep up with the intensity. That's how data has helped us – we realised that we have to give them more kilometres [to run in training] or high-intensity runs. We're now monitoring everything they do in training, and we know what they have to do in training so that they can come closer to knowing what it's like to be a first-team player and knowing the reality of what they have to face. Those things help. Then we have, of course, the physical part where we have power training, and we can monitor their growth using technology. It is something helpful for the youth.'

Playing at De Toekomst comes with a certain pressure. Once the media gains attention of a top talent, all eyes are on them. Facebook posts are made, highlights packages are shared on Instagram and analysts often share details on Twitter. It's part and parcel of a player coming through any academy and protecting them from the perils of the media is a substantial responsibility for Ajax. De Boer highlights how they're often in contact with the players' families in the hope of keeping the youngsters' feet on the ground. 'Protecting players from media hype is difficult nowadays with social media. We always give information to the boys that they're public figures as Ajax players and people want to know about them. We warn them about it and it's also a duty of the parents of players. It's very difficult – once people know about you, they may think you're a star. It's something we discuss but it's complicated to tackle. Media is a part of life, and we're always advising them on how to deal with it.'

De Toekomst is special. It's where stars are made with methods that have made legends and it's the lifeblood of Ajax. According to the CIES Football Observatory, 81 Ajax-honed players played in Europe's top 31 leagues in the 2021/22 season – more than any other club in Europe – and that is a nod to their methods. The club are associated with producing stars and in Europe there are few who can match their level of excellence in the game. Over the last few decades, Ajax have won league titles and European Cups, seen players come and go, football evolve and modernise, but the notion has always been the same: it all starts at home with the academy.

FOR EVERYONE

The foundations of Ajax Vrouwen,
with those who experienced it

THE FINAL of the Women's European Championships in 2017 was a historic event for the Netherlands. At a time when the Dutch men were struggling, having failed to qualify for Euro 2016 and were on the verge of missing out on the World Cup in 2018, the women were giving the country footballing pride. Over the course of the previous three weeks, the national team were on top form. Held in the Netherlands, the *Leeuwinnen* had a perfect record going into the final: five played, five won, nine goals scored and just one conceded. The final against Denmark was a treat of attacking football. The Netherlands won 4-2, with the likes of Vivianne Miedema and Lieke Martens heavily involved, and it resulted in the team winning their first-ever major international trophy.

The success was a watershed moment and led to more greatness in the future. Just two years later, they were World Cup finalists, falling to the supremely gifted United States of America in France. Women's football in the Netherlands was on the rise, but it was different not so long ago. In 2015, they qualified for their first-ever Women's World

Cup and reached the second round, losing to Japan. While there was praise aimed at coach Roger Reijners for leading the team to qualification, many felt as though the team had potential for more. Arjan van der Laan was Reijners's successor and even he failed to get the best out of the side. However, Sarina Wiegman's appointment as head coach in January 2017 changed things. Now, they started to play with more bravery and dominance, like how the Dutch were used to playing.

Few imagined the Dutch would go all the way at the Euros, but as they got better, the nation was more invested. For the final, 4.1 million people tuned in and 5.5 million – about a third of the country – watched the team's coronation as champions. An international football champion isn't just born – it takes years of fixing and perfecting, and that's exactly what happened in the Netherlands.

The country has a long but strained relationship with the women's game. Football has been played by women since the end of the 19th century. The first known organised women's football match in the Netherlands was in Rotterdam in 1896, although this was cancelled because of concerns over the 'good name of the sport'. There is still evidence of women playing football before 1920 as well, however, but for large periods, like many other nations, women were banned from the sport.

Between 1934 and 1955, actions were taken to prohibit women from participating in football, but soon after it would see a boom. In the following decades, more and more women would take part in the game and, in the early 1970s, FIFA, UEFA and the KNVB would finally lift the ban on women's football and recognise the Dutch women's national team.

It wasn't until 2007 that the women would have a professional league. The *Vrouwen Eredivisie* was born that year; however, it happened without the country's top teams. Six clubs took part in its inaugural competition: ADO Den Haag, AZ Alkmaar, Heerenveen, Twente, Utrecht and Willem II, with the aim of safely spreading costs, professionalising the game even further, youth development, giving the players adequate facilities and encouraging more clubs to take part in the near future. AZ dominated the initial years, winning the first three titles, while ADO Den Haag and Twente were also getting in on the act. The league still felt empty, however. The country's three biggest and most successful clubs had no part to play, and there was pressure on them to join.

By 2012, to help with funding and believing it would further help the women's game, the KNVB decided to stop their backing for the *Vrouwen Eredivisie* and push for a joint women's BeNe League – a division with the top Dutch and Belgian clubs – and it was approved by UEFA in March that year. On 18 May, Ajax decided to join in the women's football revolution. At a time when over 125,000 women and girls were playing football in the Netherlands, Ajax felt this was the right time to join in and immediately they made crucial appointments to support the team. Marleen Molenaar, formerly of AZ Alkmaar, was named the manager of the team and working under her would be head coach Ed Engelkes, the former assistant of the Dutch women's national team.

Alongside them were big signings like the national team captain, Daphne Koster, and fellow internationals Anouk Hoogendijk and Petra Hogewoning. They were mixed with some fantastic youngsters: Liza van der Most, Babiche Roof and Mandy Versteegt all signed on. Within a few weeks in the summer of 2012, a new team was created from scratch and the manner in which Ajax went about their business – picking up players from fellow Dutch clubs – didn't go down well with many. Still, the general consensus was that Ajax's presence in the women's game would be massively beneficial to the sport and community as a whole.

Molenaar, who took on most of the responsibility of the Ajax Women, explained her role and work to me: 'As manager of Ajax Vrouwen, I was responsible for setting up, implementing and managing the women's department within Ajax. First, I formed a staff and a team in a very short time. Then I had to bring everything to do with the Ajax Vrouwen to the attention of the club on all fronts. I was the first point of contact within the club and also within the staff. I was the first point of contact both inside and outside the club, and also towards the KNVB and other organisations. In addition, I had responsibilities such as submitting the budget with a justified increase in the budget for each season. This was partly to professionalise the financial conditions of the contracts with, for example, the possibility of individual sponsor deals.

'This also includes expanding the staff, training camps abroad, expanding medical aspects and much more. The sporting goal was to win the national championship and the cup every year and then to structurally connect with the top international teams. We wanted to qualify for the UEFA Women's Champions League every season with an annual progression.'

Molenaar was heavily involved in the day-to-day running of the women's team. Daughter of Cornelis 'Cees' Molenaar, who set the foundations for AZ Alkmaar in the 1960s, she herself played football for the Dutch national team and used to manage AZ, where she became national champion on three occasions before moving to Ajax.

She's passionate about her work and achievements at Ajax. To build a team from scratch isn't easy, but Molenaar managed to do it and wanted to succeed in the long run: 'The aim was to give Ajax Vrouwen a face, just like the men. To let our staff and team show that they are a full-fledged pillar of the club's sporting culture. To win the hearts of football fans with attractive, attacking and high-quality football. To bind supporters to us, to build a solid core with mutual respect and to spoil them with fresh and sparkling football at the highest level every week. All this in an attractive atmosphere, accessible to young and old. We wanted to generate support from club volunteers to radiate real unity, showing that the great Ajax are also proud to present their women to the world. We wanted to make a dream come true for many girls and women, to really be able to play football at Ajax, either in Ajax Vrouwen's senior teams or in an Ajax youth girls training programme.'

She adds: 'In general, integrating Ajax Vrouwen in a professional way within the existing organisation, which at that time was one big men's football stronghold, was one of my biggest challenges. Women's football was completely new to Ajax. It was a challenge to get the Ajax Vrouwen embraced by everything and everyone that breathes Ajax. In the start-up phase forming a new staff and team within a few weeks was my first task. My choice was Ed Engelkes as head coach on the one hand and Eva Blewanus – now involved with the men's team – as physiotherapist on the other. From there, together with the coach, I put together a team worthy of Ajax in no time. We were very much looking forward to the first league match. The team presented itself to the public in a great way in a packed De Toekomst. I think back to this historic moment with pride and goosebumps!'

Tessel Middag, who was part of that first crop of Ajax players and is currently with Scottish club Rangers, felt this was something unimaginable for her and many other girls like her: 'It was a special experience to be a part of the first group. The *Eredivisie* started in 2007 with six clubs but everyone was waiting for one of the big three in the Netherlands to start their own women's team. Ajax was eventually the first of the three back in the summer of 2012. It's the biggest club in the Netherlands, not only amongst men, but for everyone. There was a lot of buzz and a lot of players who wanted to play for Ajax, including me. I was born and bred in Amsterdam. I went to the men's games a couple of times when I was young, and I supported the team growing up in the city. For me to be able to join Ajax was a special feeling. It wasn't a dream come true because it never was a realistic dream for girls to put on the Ajax shirt. All my heroes in my youth were men – players like Wesley Sneijder and Rafael van der Vaart. They broke through when I was young, and I enjoyed watching them. I couldn't have imagined back then that less than ten years later, I would be putting on the same shirt.'

Similar thoughts are shared by her former team-mate, Leonne Stentler, currently a pundit on ESPN and NOS, who added that playing for Ajax unsurprisingly came with big, and often unrealistic, expectations: 'Everyone around the country was excited that Ajax had a women's team. The competition was already existent for five years, so Ajax had to take some players from other teams, and I know that a lot of clubs weren't happy that they did that. It was the first time clubs were allowed to contact as many players as they liked. Before that, there were some restrictions set to ensure the level of the competition was in control and that you couldn't sign all the players you wanted. With Ajax and PSV being newcomers, they really wanted to be able to sign all the players – that was the only thing they asked for. That was an interesting time and, of course, because of that, the expectations were really high, and all the clubs were keeping an eye on Ajax. They were getting top players and the expectation was that they became champions. We really felt that everyone wanted us to fail, because we were Ajax and everyone that's not associated with Ajax doesn't like Ajax.'

With a side quickly assembled, they got down to the football with friendlies against domestic sides and took part in a tournament organised by FC Twente, where they faced off against the hosts as well as Paris Saint-Germain, drawing both. It was on 24 August 2012 that they made their official debut, facing Heerenveen at De Toekomst, and the interest was palpable. Over 3,000 fans of all ages, including many of the Ajax ultras, came in to show their support. The supporters were loud, bringing in their famous Ajax songs and chants, drums and cheers and the team delivered: Desiree van Lunteren and Roof scored one each in a 2-0 win.

Middag recalls the first game well, believing that most players from that group will point out to it as their most memorable moment when they played for Ajax: 'The first game is something that will stay with me for a long time. We walked on to the pitch at De Toekomst and just to hear the club song being played while we were walking on to the pitch gave me goosebumps. Just to have so many people there –

almost a full capacity – was a magical moment. While I was walking on to the pitch, I had flashbacks to the men's games I used to watch in the Amsterdam Arena with one of my best friends in primary school. I just thought: "When those players walked on to the pitch, they had the same club song, and everyone applauded. Now, they're applauding me in my Ajax shirt." That's one of the highlights of my time there.'

The new BeNe League's format meant that in their debut season, Ajax would compete against Dutch and Belgian clubs. Before the winter break, they would compete amongst their own and if they finished in the top four, they would progress to a mix of clubs from both nations. Ajax did end up finishing fourth in the Netherlands and when the two nations mixed they finished fourth again – a respectable result for a team that was quickly formed and only had a few weeks to prepare before the start of the campaign. Although they had many national-team players and the prestige of being Ajax, it was critical for expectations to be slightly more subdued than they actually were.

The following campaign, there was a tweak in the format as all 14 clubs from both countries (seven from each) made up the league, which was won by Twente. Ajax were third. There was still a prize for them in the campaign, as they ended up winning the KNVB Cup, beating PSV 2-1 in the final as Mandy Versteegt scored twice. The improvements were slowly there and the traditional Ajax blueprint of commanding, entertaining football was evident.

As Middag put it, there was no room for any other way at Ajax: 'Right from the start, our philosophy was to play attractive, dominant and attacking football. The principles laid out by Johan Cruyff were evident. He always emphasised that if fans come to watch a game of football, it should be exciting to watch, and fans should be entertained. It didn't mean that every single game we played the 4-3-3. That changed depending on the opponent, but the concept was always clear. That was to dominate the game. It would've been strange if the women's team wore the Ajax shirt and didn't follow the Ajax philosophy. That's ingrained in every team at the club.'

The players themselves noticed a difference when they played for Ajax and the difference they were making in the community. As highlighted, women's football in the Netherlands was a late bloomer and having Ajax as a part of it was vital. It wasn't until 2009 and the European Championships that year that they had qualified for a major international tournament – that's incredibly late for a country whose men had previously played in two World Cup finals and won the Euros nearly two decades prior. For the many girls and women who were playing football in the country, having its biggest club start a team of their own created a key pathway: kids dream of playing for Ajax, now the girls could too. In their first talent day, over 900 girls took part – an indication of their popularity.

Stentler: 'There was definitely an impact on kids and parents were also interested in clubs like Ajax. When we would have a talent day, we could see how many little girls wanted to play for the club. There were so many advantages of Ajax being a big club in the men's game. All the kids wanted to play for Ajax and, because it was now possible, lots of girls could now play for them. You can only see that growing and being more normal. In the past, you would hear kids say, "I want to play for Ajax but it's not possible," but it's the opposite now and they can dream beyond just Ajax.'

Stentler continues, adding that because she now played for Ajax, more people paid more attention to women's football in the country and gave it the respect it so rightly deserves: 'I experienced higher levels of interest when I played for Ajax compared to when I played for ADO Den Haag [her previous club]. For example, I was studying when I played for my previous club and when I used to tell my colleagues at university that I couldn't be at classes because of my football, they used to tell me it was my hobby and wished me well. But when I moved to Ajax and I told them I couldn't attend classes, they used to take great interest and understood that this was a big part of my career. Even though I was already playing in the Dutch national team before I joined Ajax, people took notice and there was a big difference when I moved to Ajax. That explains why it's so important for bigger clubs to take part in women's football – interest is much higher. Our first game with Ajax, we played at De Toekomst, and the stands were full. It was so busy and so many different age groups coming to watch. We, as players, were surprised by this too.'

To Amsterdam, Molenaar brought plenty of expertise and know-how and was one of the more reputable figures in the women's game. At Ajax, her role was to make the women's team feel more of a part of the club by getting all departments to think on the same wavelength as the team and also ensuring the players had access to the best facilities.

That was one of the most positive factors about Ajax, that they made their women's side feel as integrated as possible. Molenaar did a fine job in ensuring the players felt at home, and she worked closely with those above her, mainly Marc Overmars, in keeping things well at Ajax. While Molenaar kept tabs on the football side, the final decisions, including those on budget, were made by Overmars, and most players felt they were managed well. Stentler: 'Marc Overmars was heavily involved. He was very interested in our performances, and I was injured often in my last year and a half so most of the time I was off the pitch. In that time, I would see Overmars at least once a week, coming over to our side of De Toekomst and asking if everything was alright with me and the team. He is responsible for us, and he felt responsible for us and our team performances. We would see Edwin van der Sar less, but we knew he was often involved in big decisions. He tried to make the team feel more integrated within the club. They were treating us really well.'

Molenaar adds to this as well, telling me it was the effort of the group that made the women's team better: 'I was appointed by Henri van der Aat, who was the director at Ajax at the time. He left the club after a short time and some time later, Edwin van der Sar and Marc Overmars joined. They had a lot to deal with, so they decided to focus on their core business. It was interesting to bring attention to a completely new branch, which appeared so suddenly, in a responsible and tactical way. The support of my colleagues grew steadily, and I received the full confidence of the management. Overmars gave support where he could, and also saw a future in women's football. I also have to mention Menno Geelen, who has been commercial director for a few years now, and Hennie Heinrichs, who was then the chairman.'

Middag feels the respect given to the women's team was helpful and, having seen the situations at other clubs with regards to women's football, Ajax having the right personnel was beneficial to the women's side: 'I've been in four different countries, and I've experienced it [treatment of women's teams]. It is always necessary to have the right people on board who are eager to improve women's football and it takes a while before people understand the difficulties and background of the women's game. There needs to be more understanding of how to best go forward. In our first years at Ajax, there was the matter of us trying to cement our place within the organisation and gain a bigger voice at the club. It's often the same in the women's game – there's always a fight for access to grass pitches instead of Astroturf, access to the gym and those things. It's good to see how the facilities are improving every year. Ajax is on the right track and it's particularly exciting that the club is going to build a mini stadium where the women's team and B team will play their home games.'

Ajax were under the leadership of coach Engelkes, who had previously worked with the Dutch national team as an assistant between 2004 and 2012 while also managing AZ Alkmaar between 2007 and 2012. It was in 2012 when the opportunity arose to move to Ajax and, having had good links with Molenaar, he was given the head coach gig. Engelkes did important work for Ajax, taking the new team to challenge the top, and after the BeNe League was dissolved in 2015 and the *Eredivisie* made a return, the objective was to go all the way. That chance came in the 2016/17 season, when Engelkes, in his final campaign as manager, won the league and cup double. This would also prove to be the final Ajax campaign for veterans Hoogendijk and Koster, who would go on to work with the upper management of the women's team.

At Euro 2017, five Ajax players were selected for the Dutch squad – Van Lunteren, Stefanie van der Gragt, Sisca

Folkertsma, Kelly Zeeman and Liza van der Most, with the first two starting in the successful final – while one, Davina Philtjens, represented Belgium. It was a testament to how far they had come in just five years after starting off that there were six players participating in a major tournament. Two years later at the World Cup, four Ajax players were part of the side that reached the final with the Netherlands and three Ajax players played at the Summer Olympics in Tokyo for the 2020 Games. Ajax were now a hub for players looking to improve their international prospects.

Following Euro 2017, Engelkes was replaced by Benno Nihom, his former assistant, and he would be the man in charge of leading them in the Champions League, where they reached the round of 32 before falling to Italy's Brescia. That year, Molenaar left her role as well, and former player Koster took over the reins, hoping to use her playing experience to take the team forward. Nihom would help Ajax retain the *Eredivisie* title and also win the cup, where the Amsterdam side would establish a dynasty. In his final season, 2018/19, the cup was won again but they were embarrassed in the Champions League by Lyon, the standard-bearers in European women's football. The French side beat Ajax 13-0 on aggregate in the round of 16. Additionally, the league title was also lost.

Since then, under coach Danny Schenkel, the hunt for the league title has gone on but the Eredivisie Cup, created in 2019, has found its way, with Ajax winning the 2020/21 edition. Ajax are headed in the right direction – they've got a firm playing philosophy and the finances to match, but more could be done to solidify their position as the top team in the Netherlands. Just like in the men's game, the appeal of playing for other European clubs always lingers, and perhaps their recruitment is still lacking.

What can be the long-term ambition for Ajax Vrouwen? Molenaar: 'After establishing a stable, professional branch in the five and a half years that I was there, I saw many opportunities to build a qualitative organisation. The road to this was not always easy, but with a lot of positive vibes, driven commitment and ultimate passion, a solid foundation has been laid. There was a completely new department at the time, which not only won over all souls within the club, but also a national championship and KNVB Cup. Now that the management is also increasingly saying that the time is ripe to take even more steps, I look to the future very positively. Just like with the men, Ajax want to train our own youth players to the top. Additionally, they want to supplement the team with experienced internationals as a balance and always bring crowd-pleasing players like a Lieke Martens to Amsterdam. In my time, a transfer to Barcelona took precedence, but I would like to reserve her number anyway.'

Ajax aren't quite at the heights of Barcelona, Chelsea or Lyon in the women's game, but within their own capacity, there could arguably be more room for improvement. Still, their work in their first decade was very much needed. At a time when women's football is getting better, and more women play the sport than ever before, especially in the Netherlands, an outlet such as theirs was essential.

MELODIES PURE AND TRUE
Media, social media and friends abroad

CARDIFF AND Ajax have a great connection. It was here that Ajax and its fans developed an affection for Bob Marley's 1980 hit, 'Three Little Birds', and the song has been synonymous with them ever since. On 1 August 2008, Ajax travelled to Cardiff for a friendly against Cardiff City at Ninian Park. The match was hardly eventful, ending 0-0, but the scenes after the game created an everlasting legacy. With local police fearful that there could be fan trouble after the match, they asked the hosts to keep the Ajax fans in the stadium for a little longer until it was emptier for them to move. To keep them entertained, stadium announcer Ali Yassine played a few songs, including a lot of reggae, and one particular hit made him a favourite.

That was Marley's 'Three Little Birds', and it struck a chord with the travelling supporters, who were now having a party in South Wales, singing and clapping throughout. From Cardiff, that song went everywhere with Ajax. It took over a year to arrive to the Amsterdam Arena – first being sung against Dinamo Zagreb in October 2009 – but since then it has become a part of the furniture at the club, through good and bad. From Old Trafford in Manchester

251

in 2012 to Celtic Park in Glasgow in 2015, the Friends
Arena in Stockholm in 2017 to the Santiago Bernabéu in
Madrid in 2019 and, of course, the Johan Cruyff Arena,
the song has followed Ajax and its supporters everywhere.
Marley's son, Ky-Mani, also got wind of it and became a fan
of Ajax. He was invited to watch their league match against
Emmen in August 2018, admitting it would be a dream to
sing the famous song with the rest of the fans at the Johan
Cruyff Arena.

'My father was a big football fan, and football and
the music went hand in hand,' Ky-Mani explained to
Bleacher Report. Soon, he would get his wish and, before
a Champions League match against AEK Athens, he
performed 'Three Little Birds' with the Ajax faithful in
Amsterdam. 'Being able to perform the song there, to feel
the energy and the vibration there that day, did something
to me I'll never forget. Ajax, that's my team. From now until
the day my number is gone,' he later said. Marley's daughter
Cedella also added: 'I am beyond touched that Ajax has
taken "Three Little Birds" and made it their anthem. Stories
like this warm my heart and show how impactful songs like
"Three Little Birds" can be. Soccer was everything to my
father … and to use his words, "football is freedom".'

In many ways, 'Three Little Birds' was symbolic of
21st century Ajax – the lyrics express a message of hope
and motivation, and it stuck with Ajax through thick and
thin. It's also reflective of the free spirit in the city. From
the Velvet Revolution to the current day, the song has
been an ever-present, and as the club hoped, it became
popular internationally as well. Ajax's brilliant Europa
League and Champions League runs in 2017 and 2019
respectively made videos of fans collectively singing the

song go viral, and it gave people abroad an affinity with the club.

In 2021, ahead of the start of the new season in August, Ajax released their third kit and paid homage to Marley and 'Three Little Birds'. Kit sponsor Adidas produced a black shirt with the famous three stripes on the side in the colours of the Rasta flag: green, yellow and red. On the back, sitting on the Saint Andrew's Cross, were three birds, once again in those colours. It was a tribute to the connection Marley and the song had developed in recent times and it became popular with the fans, selling out in record time with orders and demand for the shirt continuously on the rise.

I spoke to James Webb from Adidas, who works with Ajax on their designs, and he explained a bit about the shirt that caught the eye of fans the world over: 'We knew about the fairly new fans' tradition of singing "Three Little Birds" at games and were compelled to find out if we could create a product that could be cool and tell that story. Adidas has a history with Bob Marley: he wore the three stripes a few times, and he also loved football. Historically, as a brand, we've created apparel, track tops, jackets inspired by this iconic colour story, the Rasta flag and the black base. It's an iconic look of Adidas also and when we had the chance to mix that with this story and have Ajax play it on the biggest platform of the Champions League, then we couldn't pass that up.'

Webb also spoke about Adidas's relationship with Ajax as a whole, explaining how intensively the club are involved and open to creative ideas: 'We are very proud of our long and creative relationship with Ajax, that has spanned across two decades and has evolved into a very global partnership. Ajax are incredibly open-minded and constantly looking to explore new territories to expand our partnership. We work as a global design and product creation team with our Adidas colleagues in Amsterdam. Edwin van der Sar and his team are involved in every meeting and are always very open and creative. This transparent approach from the top down has definitely facilitated and fostered a really good relationship between us and we really look forward to our meetings and every project we have with Ajax. We can't speak for the club, but we can say we have a meeting of minds now, and we are very happy to be able to work so open and collaboratively with Ajax. They have a receptive mindset to doing new things. They see the excitement and chance to move into new territories together and create a leading approach to building beautiful products.'

Webb adds to this, explaining the thought process behind some of Ajax's most iconic kits in recent years, including the away shirt from the 2018/19 season that saw victories against Real Madrid, Juventus and Tottenham in the Champions League: 'The 2018/19 away shirt was an interesting design season. On home shirts, we always respect the iconic red colour blocking, but there is a history on away shirts of bold colour blocks also, especially dating back to the great era of the 90s. That was a time of progressive and free design expression. There were a variety of styles and blockings, but they were part of the graphic and visual identity of those great kits, which became iconic. For this kit we created a design that paid into those great kits but in a modern way by mixing up the colour palette – another feature of Ajax away kits. The colours were new for the club and influenced by what was going on in streetwear and youth culture at the time, combining the most worn and commercial black base and then accented with white and a beige-gold colour. This was something that linked into our creative direction at the time of products that are wearable in any environment, whether in the stadium or on the streets.'

Additionally, when Ajax reintroduced their classic crest used between 1928 and 1990 for their 2021/22 home kits, the shirt was widely adored for its nod to heroes of the past and Webb thinks it's symbolic: 'The home kit is an icon: we are highly respectful of the history of this shirt so we work closely with the club and identify the details we can work on and within to make it new and exciting each season. For 2021/22, we quickly realised that by reintroducing the crest used between 1928 and 1990, it would become a symbol of unity, uniting generations of fans and families together. We in turn toned down our three-stripe branding contrast and created a very simplistic, reduced and contemporary iteration of the iconic home shirt.'

In the modern day, a great shirt and club requires a great team behind the scenes to promote it and in 2021 Ajax have one of the most innovative teams working on their media and social media content, enhancing the club even further in this digital age. With over 30 employees managing their social media, television and print output, covering the men's and women's first team as well as youth sides of all ages, they do their best to promote the club even further and share their success with the world. The media department has six core objectives to follow, centred around boosting the club and image of the city they are based in:

1. Attacking thinking

2. Showing leadership

3. Wanting to be the best

4. Directed towards Amsterdam

5. Bringing talent to fruition

6. Reinforcing each other

Some may take it for arrogance, but it is true that to be a part of Ajax, you have to show that you are willing to be the best – and that applies to the media department as well. Working in the media team is Miel Brinkhuis, the club's head of communications, along with Daan Germans, the editor-in-chief, and under them are a specialist team who prioritise each popular social media platform. As of October 2021, Ajax are the most followed team in the Netherlands. On Twitter, they've got 1.4 million followers; on Facebook, their official page has 3.3 million likes; on Instagram, they have 6 million followers; on YouTube, they've got 806,000 subscribers; and on TikTok, they've got 3.3 million followers. All of this is at least three times more than that of their nearest rivals, PSV Eindhoven and Feyenoord.

While Ajax have been actively involved in promoting their media image since 2009, it wasn't until the 2016/17 season that they reached a different level, becoming one of the best clubs in the world in that regard. That season, their reinvented strategy saw them working actively with stunning documentaries and hysterical GIFs, appealing to a wider audience ranging across various age groups. Ajax's run to the Europa League Final caught the eye of many thanks to their wonderful football and youthfulness and, ahead of the final in Stockholm, the club had a clear message to send out: they were back. They made a video to match it. Released on 24 May 2017, the morning of the final, the video started: 'Dear Europe, welcome to our dream. I bet you still know us,' before proceeding to remind everyone of who they are – a club that prides itself on youth and creativity, and adding in tributes to Johan Cruyff, who had died a year prior.

The video, which was just over a minute long, was titled 'We Are Back' – and in context, they were right. Ajax hadn't gone this far in a European competition in over two decades, but it felt as though the title bit them back. They lost to Manchester United in the final, and just a few months later were knocked out of Europe entirely in the 2017/18 season, failing to reach the group stages of both the Champions League and Europa League. It's possible to get things wrong in this line of work – social media is volatile, but more often than not, Ajax get it so right and they do it beautifully. With the inconsistent results in the 2017/18 season combined with the sadness around the club after Abdelhak Nouri's collapse, that campaign proved to be one to forget, but like how Ajax's transfer policy changed in the summer of 2018, the media promotions were at their best too.

With the signings of Dušan Tadić and Daley Blind, Ajax's media department produced creative videos to announce their arrivals. For Tadić, they referenced the city's history with famous works of art, labelling the Serbian forward as an artist with the football and giving fans a hint of what he's set to bring to Amsterdam. With Blind's return, they took advantage of that summer's World Cup and England's run to the semi-final. The video *Daley's Coming Home* was released. It was an imitation of David Baddiel, Frank Skinner and the Lightning Seeds' song, 'Three Lions', and it once again referenced the recent history of Ajax: the 30th league title, which got them the third star above their crest, the four-year title drought they were on and Blind's finest moments for Ajax in his first stint.

Perhaps their best work came in the Champions League run that season, especially after the group stages as Ajax went on an unlikely journey to the semi-finals. Ahead of the second leg against Real Madrid, there was a tear-jerker. A poignant two-minute clip showed three top Ajax talents, Donny van de Beek, Kasper Dolberg and Hakim Ziyech, receiving phone calls from their family members. Van de Beek got a call from his father and they discussed a young Donny's dreams of playing for Ajax as well his first visit to the Amsterdam Arena as a child. Dolberg got a call from his sister, telling him what it was like when he first moved to Amsterdam from Denmark. Ziyech's brother reminded him that this was the sort of stage he belonged at. All three had the same message: their dreams were now, and they should enjoy it. It was emotional. So pure and so beautiful. Ajax then went on to win 4-1, and although the video didn't play a part in the football, it told the story of Ajax as a club – the unity and connection was unmatched.

Before their quarter-final clash against Juventus, Ajax took bits from Dutch DJ Armin van Buuren's hit, 'Blah Blah Blah'. Amidst online chatter that Ajax were lucky to get this far, having beaten a depleted Real Madrid team, and that they would be knocked out by Juventus, who were amongst the top favourites to win the Champions League, the intention of the video was to prove that the team didn't care about what others said to negate their achievements and that they were focused on the task in hand, using their quality, motivation from their glorious past and the undeniable class they had showed on their run so far. Ajax, once again, won the tie against the odds, beating Juventus 3-2 on aggregate. On the pitch, they were brilliant, and on social media, the media department were matching the team.

Ahead of the Tottenham semi-final, there were clips praising the fans' support, the team's run thus far, tributes to former Ajax players Christian Eriksen, Jan Vertonghen and Toby Alderweireld, and even though the semi-final ended in heart-wrenching fashion for Ajax, the campaign was wonderful. The numbers were there to back up how the good work put in by the media team was. On 10 May 2019, the day after the second-leg semi-final defeat, they had 2.9 million likes on their Facebook page (a rise of 17.5 per cent compared with 1 July 2018), on Instagram it was 2.3 million (a rise of 215 per cent), on Twitter they had 1.1 million followers (a rise of 15 per cent) and the number of subscribers on YouTube was 460,000 (a rise of 75 per cent).

With the exodus of players on the horizon, Ajax, who in the previous summer convinced their top stars to stay at the club for another season, now made emotional videos and social media content for their departing players. When Frenkie de Jong's move to Barcelona was confirmed, the hashtag #FrenkieFuturo was released, with Ajax asking the Catalan club to enjoy the future with the midfielder. For Matthijs de Ligt after his move to Juventus, it was #GoldenBye and the promotion of his achievements at a young age for Ajax. For Ziyech's move to Chelsea a year later, the club released a video of the Moroccan at the *Theater Tuschinski*, watching a film of his best bits at the club and when Van de Beek went to Manchester United, there was another touching clip of a chat with his father, discussing his career.

At times, Ajax could see the lighter side too, such as poking fun at Marc Overmars's constrained spending during their Christmas message of 2018 with a line in a poem, '*We vonden eindelijk de portemonnee van Marc Overmars*' ('We found Marc Overmars's wallet'), or when Overmars picked up his phone after the final day of the transfer window of the same year and saw missed calls from top clubs around Europe, insinuating that his club were not interested in doing business for their players. Even recently, there's still a drive to evoke emotions through their creativity and promoting their message of a structured youth-centric approach. Ahead of the first Champions League match of the 2021/22 campaign, they took 11 children to a local concrete pitch, all donning Ajax shirts with names of their current stars on their backs, showing their best moments in that competition: Ziyech's wonderfully threaded long pass against Bayern Munich, Ryan Gravenberch's first Champions League goal against Midtjylland and Lasse Schöne's free kick against Real Madrid, amongst others.

Apart from the media, Ajax have grown their relations with foreign clubs in recent times, specifically in China. Ever since he was appointed, one of Van der Sar's core goals was to improve the relationship with the country and he, along with the rest of the club, have been successful in that field in recent times. Since the start of 2018, Ajax have worked closely with Chinese club Guangzhou R&F – a partnership which benefits both. Ajax and the *Eredivisie* as a whole aren't popular in China, being gazumped by the Premier League and La Liga. It's common to see people in the country donning the shirts of clubs from Europe's top five leagues – Manchester United, Barcelona and Real Madrid are up there, while others are growing. Ajax and Guangzhou reached a different deal, though, one that used the Dutch club's best qualities.

China has long had ambitions in football with the dream of winning the World Cup by 2050. This is helped by President Xi Jingping's own ambition in the sport, as he hopes to see his country become a footballing superpower, setting the goal to have at least one football pitch per 10,000 people by 2025. The array of international transfers in the last decade brought its football some attention, but rarely any major improvement. However, now, there is much more focus on the developmental side of things, and that is where Guangzhou and Ajax's affiliation is in the spotlight. Since 2017, Ajax have been based in Meizou, some 380 kilometres away from central Guangzhou. Eventually, R&F formed a partnership with Ajax Coaching Academy – Ajax's coaching arm which collaborates with other clubs and institutions, sharing footballing expertise – and they've been working together since.

With a decade-long vision to see the club's youth improve and become of an international quality, 350 youngsters between the ages of 7 and 17 get the Ajax education every year. Leading the Ajax team in China is former Netherlands and Vitesse youth coach Edwin Petersen, and there is still influence from Amsterdam. In 2019, to show their gratitude for Ajax's work, R&F named their training stadium after Van der Sar and since 2018 they have been in a €2m-a-year contract (lasting until 2023 with the option to extend for a further five years in the future). In the same year, Ajax opened their Asia Pacific offices in Guangzhou, where they link up with the rest of their partners in Asia, namely in Japan.

Since January 2018, Ajax have been in a cooperation with Japanese club Sagan Tosu, helped by Hiroyuki Shirai, a coach who got his coaching badges in the Netherlands and worked for Ajax between 2010 and 2016 as a video analyst. He is currently employed by the KNVB, working with the country's youth teams. When Ajax wanted to find a partner club in Japan, Shirai was one of the people responsible for the task and he struck up a partnership with Sagan Tosu. Although Tosu isn't one of Japan's major cities, compared with Tokyo or Osaka, Ajax had a long-term vision linked with football and getting the best of both countries. As part of the agreement, Sagan Tosu's youth have often travelled to Amsterdam for training sessions and matches against Ajax in the Future Cup (a tournament for young players consisting of international clubs).

In addition to Japan, Ajax formed partnerships with other Asian and Oceanic clubs. In Australia, Sydney FC, where Dutch coach Han Berger – who previously worked in the Netherlands with Groningen, AZ, Utrecht and more – was the technical director, entered a collaboration with Ajax. In 2018, Sydney participated in the Future Cup and have been in close contact with Ajax. Since then, the two have constantly shared ideas, resources, staff and their vision on the game. In the United Arab Emirates in 2020, then champions Sharjah FC entered an agreement, once again centred around long-term growth. Away from Asia, Ajax opened their first offices in the United States in 2018 with the view of improving their status across the pond, like their European rivals have.

In all these activities, there is obvious financial gain and it's a huge part of the success of Van der Sar and chief commercial officer Menno Geelen. Whether it's their trendy Adidas shirts or their creative social media work or making football friends abroad, it's all part of the job to grow the Ajax vision and compete with Europe's best. As often highlighted, growth for a club outside Europe's top five leagues is far more difficult than for those within, but Ajax are slowly mastering the art.

WHO IS AJAX?

The glorious reinvention of Ajax

SPEAKING TO *The Guardian* in 2020, Edwin van der Sar talked about how Ajax needed to become Ajax once again. How they needed to be recognised for what they are all about and how it was important for a newer generation of fans: 'The Ajax shirt is one of the few that never change, it's the red down the middle, it's vertical, it's not horizontal, it's not in blocks,' he said. 'The main thing is to make sure that everybody knew the shirt again. In the 1970s, we had Cruyff, in the '80s we had Rijkaard and Van Basten and in the mid-90s, it was myself, Rijkaard for the second time, the De Boer twins, Davids, Seedorf, Kluivert, Overmars. And after that period it was a little bit quiet. So for us it was to have a new younger audience to know: "Who is Ajax?"'

In context, Van der Sar was discussing how he wanted fans abroad to have a soft spot for Ajax, but a lot of what he said could be related to by Ajax fans in their home city. It's well known by now: Ajax had lost their way, had become a club that was unrecognisable by their own and had a successful resurgence. Over the years, this also helped repair a connection that seemed lost – a strong relationship between the club and its fans. Ajax weren't historically known to be close to their supporters, but in this new era they tried to be different, and that, in turn, has contributed to their success.

'Johan Cruyff stepped in, and his idea was to have former players on the board,' says Fabian Nagtzaam, the managing director of the *Supportersvereniging Ajax* (Ajax Supporters' Association), reminding me of the start of Johan Cruyff's revolution. 'The connection with the fans immediately got better because those people – Marc Overmars, Dennis Bergkamp, Wim Jonk and the others – knew what it was like to play for us. Before that [the revolution], we had bank directors and others in charge of the club. They had no connection with us fans like how Overmars and Edwin van der Sar do. There's been a lot of changes over the last decade, but that connection is the biggest one. Before that, Ajax were seen as a "cold" club – not very involved with the fans. I've been watching Ajax for 35 years and we all know the great success with Louis van Gaal and a young team. That was great, and part of that team were Overmars and Van der Sar, and when they returned to the club in their current roles, they wanted to copy that mid-90s success and bring it to the modern day.'

How have Ajax made an effort to be closer with their fans? By welcoming them with open arms, Nagtzaam says. They've been more open to dialogue and having discussions, and even little gestures make a difference. 'They're always talking to us,' Nagtzaam adds, bringing up a recent instance. 'When there's a matter to deal with, they're always discussing it with us. There was recently a great example: I was at the Johan Cruyff Arena with a lot of fans. Van der Sar was there too but he was doing something else. He stopped by our group, had a chat and took pictures. They're always welcoming us with open arms. With this connection, they know our thoughts and what we want. Together, we try to make a great atmosphere in the Arena and that helps the team.'

A great example of this improved relationship came at the end of the 2020/21 season, when Ajax won their 35th league title in a season mostly played behind closed doors, where fans couldn't attend matches, missing out on 30 of their 34 league games. To commemorate their fans' support, Ajax burned their *Eredivisie* shield and made championship stars, each weighing 3.45 grams and containing 0.06 grams of the actual shield to give to all their season ticket holders. They ended up making 42,390 stars, and produced a video where Ajax players Dušan Tadić, Ryan Gravenberch and Lisandro Martínez were in a tin foundry, melting the title. In the same video, Marc Overmars, carrying two briefcases, was shown walking out to the city, insinuating he was out to deliver the stars. Accompanied by Maggie MacNeal's Eurovision hit from 1980 titled 'Amsterdam', the artistic nature of the video and overall gesture was praised worldwide.

'This season, we have largely had to play without our fans. Well, without them sitting in the stands, at least,' Van der Sar said about the gesture. 'Despite this, we have felt their support every week. On the way to the stadium, on social media and in our personal contacts. Previously, when we said, "This title is for you," we were expressing how we were doing it for the fans; however, sharing the trophy is the ultimate proof that we really are. After a turbulent year, we are ensuring our fans feel part of our championship.'

Another fan, Rodney Rijsdijk, tells me about how Ajax are now more 'warm' to their supporters: 'We saw ourselves more as customers than as fans. The feeling that we should be glad that we may go to watch Ajax was gone. Ajax improved itself as a warmer club in the years later. More dialogue between supporters and fans, more appreciation for our support, sometimes really nice gifts for our season ticket holders.' Little gestures go a long way. In a time when the top level of European football is so distant from its supporters, having a club like Ajax do things differently is refreshing.

The improvement of Ajax has led to greater pride in the Ajax shirt as well. More people, especially younger ones, follow Ajax in Amsterdam than they did before. The club's shirt is visible in most places, replacing the old times where they followed Europe's other top clubs first and Ajax second. Nagtzaam: 'The Arena is changing as well – it's more of an Ajax stadium. Before, it was also for concerts and other events. The seats are now of the red of Ajax having had all sorts of colours previously. There are more pictures of former players around the stadium. It became more Ajax. Indeed, a lot of children are interested. Ten or 15 years ago, we used to see children wearing shirts of other clubs like Barcelona or other big clubs across Europe. Nowadays, however, they're proud to wear the Ajax shirt again.'

In addition to the increased number of children taking interest in Ajax, the different cultures following Ajax is great for the club to see. Amsterdam is a really multicultural city, a melting pot of different backgrounds and a place for diversity. It's common to see people from Morocco, Suriname and Turkey settle in the Dutch capital, and many of them follow Ajax. For the Moroccans, Amsterdam is their city of settlement in the Netherlands. In the past, it was common to see Moroccan footballers find their way at

Ajax in Amsterdam, even though they may not have been born or raised in the city. Think of the likes of Mounir El Hamdaoui, Ismaïl Aissati, Nourdin Boukhari or Anwar El Ghazi, who have all played for Ajax in the 21st century. That continued into recent times, where the likes of Hakim Ziyech and Noussair Mazraoui have become incredibly popular, while Abdelhak Nouri has become the son of Ajax and Amsterdam.

Nouri, born in Amsterdam and having gone through the system at De Toekomst, was touted as one of Ajax's biggest stars and was destined for great things at the club. He made his debut for the senior team in September 2016 but his cardiac arrhythmia attack in a friendly against Werder Bremen in Austria on 8 July 2017 saddened the club and its fans. Over the years, despite having recently made his debut for the first team before his incident, he had become a favourite because of his cheerful, joyous nature. In the spring of 2017, he did an 'internship' with the Ajax media team and his experiences were highlighted in a short documentary series, which is still available to view on Ajax's YouTube channel. In the videos, he's seen performing pranks, laughing around, working with Ajax's fan support services and interviewing Ajax figures, including then captain Davy Klaasen.

The videos told a lot about Nouri's personality and how loved he was around the club, and just like those within Ajax, the fans were hurt after the incident as well. Nagtzaam: 'Just saying his name gives me goosebumps. Appie is one of us. He's from Amsterdam. He had his education at De Toekomst. When it happened, we all came together. We were all one. Fans from other clubs joined in and knew what was going on. We still honour him. It was a big shock for all of us when it happened in Austria.' Rijsdijk adds on: 'Every fan was truly devastated and heartbroken. Not only was he one of our biggest talents, but he was also a really nice person. Look at his vlogs on YouTube. Anyone who has anything to do with Ajax loves him because of his adorable character. The day after his accident, hundreds of people came together in front of his house in Amsterdam-West. Even the non-religious Dutch fans prayed together with the Moroccans. We were all one in our sorrow.'

The performances by Ziyech and Mazroaui, especially in the 2018/19 season, as well as Nouri's attack made Ajax more of a default club with its Moroccan population and such was the affection for Nouri that even after players left Ajax they wanted to pay tribute to their friend. Donny van de Beek, who grew up with Nouri in the youth teams, took on the number 34 – Nouri's old number with the Ajax first team – when he joined Manchester United. After Van de Beek's move to England was confirmed, Nouri's father, Mohammed, explained his son's joy for his friend: 'Appie's eyes looked very sharp suddenly, he had tears of joy on his cheeks and was clearly moved when he heard Donny's voice. Donny is like a son to us. Everyone at our house was very emotional and happy with Donny's wonderful transfer. It was a special day.'

Like Van de Beek, other former Ajax and Dutch players such as Justin Kluivert at Roma, Joël Veltman at Brighton and Amin Younes at Napoli took the number 34 as a tribute to the teenager. The fans show their support for him too. On his 24th birthday on 2 April 2021, several Ajax ultras turned up outside the Nouri family home to show their support and wish him well, singing songs and lighting flares. The family were involved too, with his father holding a banner of his shirt number. He truly does have a place in the hearts of many supporters, and their frequent gestures prove how much the youngster means to Ajax.

A lot of modern Ajax is dedicated to Nouri, and a lot of it is dedicated to another hero, Cruyff, who started this all. Cruyff's career in the game came as a result of perseverance and grit. His biographer, Auke Kok, once wrote about how he was fed plenty to bulk up the flying winger and how he suffered from nervousness when he was younger. Ajax also did more for him than any other talent coming through the academy, and he was also given more punishments than any other player. Even Rinus Michels was tough on him, and that gave the game the legend we now know. Perhaps that's the embodiment of the Ajax of this era: it's been built through trial and error, through struggles and success. It's almost poetic that it took a jolt from Cruyff himself to help Ajax recognise themselves again. Cruyff's death in March 2016 was a sad event for football. It's not an exaggeration to suggest that he may arguably be the most famous Dutch person ever, and the tributes for him following his death showed how much he was appreciated, especially in Amsterdam.

Rijsdijk recalls Cruyff's legacy in Amsterdam, and how a meeting with him left him captivated for years: 'Cruyff was bigger than everything. Even bigger than Ajax. I saw grown men cry like they lost their father. Most of them did not ever meet him, but I met him twice: once at the opening day of the Amsterdam Arena which is now named after him. I used to work there as a steward and he asked me where he could find a certain parking space. As an Amsterdammer, I'm not that star-struck by famous people but Cruyff was out of that category. I told him where he had to walk. It meant nothing for him, but I was confused for days! Years later I met him in the Olympic Stadium and went on a picture with him. That picture is still hanging big in my living room.'

In 2018, several Ajax fans got together to raise €75,000 over a three-month period for a statue of Cruyff outside the Johan Cruyff Arena. Sculpted by Hans Jouta, it shows Cruyff in action in his Ajax shirt and his famous number 14 and was unveiled by Frank Rijkaard along with a host of supporters in August 2020. Although his stint as advisor ended bitterly in 2015, there was no doubt over his legacy and how much he meant to the club and the city.

'Who is Ajax?' one may ask. This is Ajax. A new Ajax. A modern Ajax. One that we hadn't seen for long but many previously enjoyed. They aren't similar to the old ones, or exactly in the way Cruyff would've wanted, but that is what makes it unique. They've got different people in charge doing things in a different way, but with the same essence of the Ajax of old. It's in the bricks and mortar of their walls to be successful, but they also have to be smart, innovative, paying attention to their own and growing sustainability.

The story of Ajax in the 21st century has been an eventful one: from drastic declines to confusion, infighting to sackings, gaffes and blissful belly flops, a resurgence and the beautiful triumphs they have had in recent years. This was the glorious reinvention of a storied football club – one that had let football go too far away, but one that recovered in a shrewd, unique way.

BIBLIOGRAPHY

NEWSPAPERS, MAGAZINES AND ONLINE SOURCES

Ajax Daily
Ajax Showtime
Ajax USA
Algemeen Dagblad
Bleacher Report
CNN
Catenaccio.nl
Consultancy.nl
De Telegraaf
De Volkskrant
Deutsche Welle
Financial Times
FourFourTwo
Goal
Het Parool
Marketing Week
NOS
NRC Handelsblad

Panorama
Revu
SportsPro Media
The Athletic
The Guardian
The Independent
These Football Times
Trouw
Tubantia
Voetbal International
Voetbal Primeur
Vrij Nederland
We Talk Ajax
World Soccer

BOOKS AND REFERENCES

Born, E., *The Velvet Revolution,* The Blizzard, Issue Fourteen, September 2014

Coronel commission, *Rapport Onderzoekcommissie, 10 Jaar Belied Ajax*, February 2008

Cruyff, J., *My Turn: The Autobiography*, Macmillan, October 2016

Kuper, S. and Szymanski, S., *Soccernomics,* Harper Sport, May 2012

Meijer, M., *Louis van Gaal: The Biography*, Ebury Press, July 2015

Pot, M., *Het Nieuwe Ajax*, Ambo | Anthos, October 2019

Winner, D., *Brilliant Orange: The Neurotic Genius of Dutch Football*, Bloomsbury Publishing, March 2001

Also available at all good book stores

9781801501125

9781801500005

9781785318870

9781785319877

9781785318702

9781785317965

9781801500500

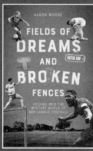

9781801501002

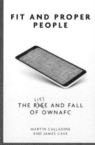

9781801500470